M000009804

It's a Dog's World

It's a Dog's World

THE SAVVY GUIDE TO FOUR-LEGGED LIVING

Wendy Diamond

BALLANTINE BOOKS / NEW YORK

Published in the United States by Ballantine Books, an imprint of The Random House Publishing Group, a division of Random House, Inc., New York.

Library of Congress Cataloging-in-Publication Data

Diamond, Wendy.
It's a dog's world: the savvy guide to four-legged living/Wendy Diamond.
p. cm.
ISBN 978-0-345-51445-5
eBook ISBN 978-0-345-51692-3
1. Dog's—Behavior. 2. Human–animal relationships. I. Title.
SF433.D52 2010
636.7—dc22
2009044542

Printed in the United States of America on acid-free paper

www.ballantinebooks.com

2 4 6 8 9 7 5 3 1

First Edition

Book design by Susan Turner

Contents

INTRODUCTION

Living in a Dog's World

Throughout my career of wet noses, puppy-dog eyes, and games of tug-of-war, I have come to one sure realization: Puppy love *does* exist. For centuries the love, loyalty, and commitment that we have given to dogs has been nothing compared to the unconditional love, loyalty, and commitment they have given us.

If someone had told me over two dog years ago (you do the math), when I was in college in Boston, that I would one day grow up to be the woman who coined the term "pet lifestyle," I would have done one of two things. I would either have laughed hysterically (I was a teenage girl; what *didn't* make me laugh hysterically back then?) or asked, "What the heck is a pet lifestyle?" (I'm from Chagrin Falls, Ohio. If my mother had heard me say anything stronger than "heck" she would have washed my mouth out with soap.) Back when I was growing up, most people named their dog Spot, and poor Spot spent most of his time outdoors and slept in a backyard doghouse. We took our pets for granted; we thought lavishing them with extra care and attention was, well, for the dogs. There was no such thing as a pet lifestyle because people didn't think of their pets as a big part of their lives. But now that we've reached the twenty-first century, in my opinion, a new pet revolution has begun (barkin' about a revolution . . . we all want to change the world).

When I graduated from college I still hadn't received my pet calling. I submitted about four hundred résumés to the companies where I thought I wanted to work, none of which thought they wanted me to work there. At a loss, I brushed off my shoulder pads and did the obvious thing: I moved to Russia to sell designer clothing. After a few years overseas, though, I'd had had enough of diplomats, last season's Valentinos, and Red Squares (of both the architectural and human variety) so I came to New York, where I hoped to find more meaning in life. And, while I was at it, maybe a job. Little did I know that I was about to go from being the underdog to rescuing the underdog—literally!

When I first set foot in New York City, I entered an entirely different dog show. New York City was no Chagrin Falls, no Boston, and certainly *nyet* Russia. With such a diverse population of Manhattanites in the city, I didn't know where I would fit in. I started to feel shallow. I knew I wanted to help those in need, but I didn't know how. I did know, however, that I was in the right place: Somehow on a tiny island crammed with millions of people, the less fortunate are easier to see than in some other places. I began volunteering for the Coalition for the Homeless, serving and delivering meals from the back of a truck. It felt great to give back, but I wanted to do more. While working with the homeless, I was lucky enough to launch two best-selling cookbooks, *A Musical Feast* and *An All-Star Feast*, with recipes from some of the top musicians and athletes of our time, including Madonna, Cher, Tony Bennett, Michael Jordan, Mickey Mantle, and Derek Jeter, with over a half-million dollars in profits from the recipe books donated to various homeless organizations.

As I continued to work with the homeless, though, I began noticing a trend. I saw that the people I was trying to help—the ones we think of as less fortunate—tended to feel a lot more fortunate when they had animal companions. They seemed to look at life differently. They had a different demeanor. The bond they shared with their four-legged pals was infectious, and I wanted in on it. Before you could say "woof woof," I headed over to Animal Care and Control, one of the top rescue facilities in Manhattan, where I saw rooms and rooms filled with loving animals without homes. It was then and there that I decided I wanted to help rescue and shelter animals. I left the shelter after adopting Pasha, my Russian blue (an homage to my days in Russia), but I was so enlivened by my new passion that I quickly came back to adopt Lucky, my Maltese, and to this day my canine best friend.

With my two new buddies in tow, I immediately dedicated myself to my new cause. I begged, rolled over, whimpered, and whined for enough money to start *Animal Fair,* the original pet-lifestyle (there's that phrase again!) magazine and website, dedicated to promoting fairness to animals, responsible breeding, and animal rescue. (We realize *Vanity Fair* has a ways to go before they catch up with our chic factor, but we're looking forward to the company.) Our premiere issue featured Renée Zellweger and her late golden, Dylan, gracing the cover. This was the first magazine of its kind—a new breed, you might say—to feature a celebrity and her pet on its cover. That was just the beginning of many covers, features, and photo spreads bringing awareness to the plight of shelter animals in desperate need of homes. Now celebrating its tenth anniversary, our magazine has put the likes of President Obama, Beyoncé Knowles, Charlize Theron, Hayden Panettiere, and Serena Williams on our covers, all with their pets,

many of the animals rescued (and some of the celebrities rescued by their pets as well).

In the beginning things weren't easy. In 1999, the year *Animal Fair* began, nearly twelve million animals were killed in the American shelter system. The pet market was about as bustling as a small New England town on the ocean. In winter. Only two designers were designing pet apparel, dog grooming products were scarce, the Sherpa Bag was the only official airline-approved dog bag, and EL AL of Israel was the only airline to offer a pet mileage program. *Oy vey!*

But then we hit the twenty-first century and everything changed. Pet boutiques started popping up like Starbarks, designer brands started launching the ultimate in haute canine couture dog product lines, hotels and spas added pet-friendly programs, and the number of pet-inspired establishments continues to grow. But our work hasn't influenced just the pet market. I'm proud to say that today, ten years after our launch, fewer than five million animals are being euthanized each year—and this number drops annually. I'd like to think that the steady decline has something to do with my continuous work profiling outstanding underdog shelters, revolutionizing dog-friendly charity events, and never giving up. And through it all my dear Lucky has contributed to helping rescue her fellow canines in distress by remaining my loyal sidekick through every hoop we've jumped through!

In 2007, *Forbes* crowned me the "Canine Queen," the *New Yorker* appointed me "the Martha Stewart of the bone and milk dish!" and the *New York Post* quipped, "Wendy Diamond is the Pet Diva!" Okay, I'm tooting my own horn, but you get the picture. All these kudos didn't happen overnight. It took a decade of sneaking Lucky into no-dog zones, dressing her up for charity, depositing her reverently into the arms of celebrities, and following her to animal rescue events all over the world to bring you this book. So I hope you enjoy it, because I wouldn't trade these past ten years working with animals for anything in the world. The phrase "pet lifestyle" is about much more than doggy spas and designer carriers. It also refers to a commitment to do what you can for animals who need rescuing—to look after the underdog, whether purebred or mutt.

It's a Dog's World

Puppercise

One day last spring, as I picked Lucky up to put her in her doggie bag, I realized two things: First, her hair was too shaggy for the coming summer months, and second, she felt a little heavy. Obviously, her extra locks were weighing her down. But when I picked her up from the groomer later that afternoon looking oh-so-cool in her puppy cut, I realized she was still heavier than usual. With a gulp, I realized the truth: The excess poundage was not because of her excess hair after all, but because little Lucky was actually a little overweight. Now, an extra pound or two may not sound like a big deal, but when you're only six or seven pounds it's like adding 15 to 30 percent to your body mass. Needless to say, immediately I put Lucky on a new diet and exercise regimen; after some thought, I went on one too (only to keep her company, you understand, not because I needed it, because I *absolutely* didn't).

If you and your dog want to live in harmony for a long, long time, you cannot be couch potatoes. Of course, you can still enjoy time together on the couch, even eating the occasional potato chip—none for the dog—but if that butt-shaped groove on your comfy couch is getting a little too groovy, it's high time you and your best friend get some puppercise. In this chapter, Lucky and I will discuss pet (and human) obesity and offer tips on how to prevent your dog from packing on the ounces. We'll also share advice on how to encourage your dog's inner athlete, help you decide which foods and treats are best for your buddy (somehow steak always ends up higher on Lucky's list than on mine), and give you some tips for finding a veterinarian to keep your dog in tip-top shape.

Obesity—the Good, the Bad, and the Ugly—for Humans and Pets

Let's get the bad news out of the way first. Thirty-three percent of American humans and 40 percent of American pets are obese. Obesity, whether human or animal, can lead

The Scary Facts

• It is estimated that 7.2 million dogs are obese and 26 million are overweight.

• Smaller pets can tip the scales from plump to obese with only two to three pounds of extra weight.

• Of dogs over age seven, 52.1% were found to be overweight or obese.

Sources: Journal of the American Medical Association, Journal of Nutrition.

to heart disease, diabetes, decreased life expectancy, and less effective flirting—all things you probably want to avoid. You and your dog need to be around to give each other love for many years to come!

Let's Get Physical: Exercising with Your Pet

When your dog is bored, he'll eat, because there's not a whole lot else for him to do—like you when you're watching TV and throwing back a pint of Ben & Jerry's Cherry Garcia or eating an entire bag of Cool Ranch Doritos, just to keep yourself occupied. I mean, I wouldn't know; I never do that, but

Breeds Prone to Obesity

Labrador retrievers, golden retrievers, beagles, Weimaraners, Dalmatians, basset hounds, Shetland sheepdogs (shelties), mastiffs, Saint Bernards, Great Danes, elkhounds, English springer spaniels, cocker spaniels, pugs, dachshunds, miniature schnauzers, miniature poodles, Shih Tzu, Welsh corgis, bichons frises (bichons), and cairn terriers.

When a dog is at a healthy weight, you should be able to feel his ribs, and when you view him from the top, you should be able to see a noticeable waist—sort of like viewing your sixteen-year-old svelte self in the mirror. (Let's pretend we were all svelte at sweet sixteen.)

If your dog is overweight, however, you will not be able to feel his ribs because of excess fat, and when you view him from the top, you won't be able to see a waist.

If you believe your dog is overweight, your first stop should be a veterinarian. She can help you come up with a game plan to whip him back into shape, as well as ruling out underlying causes for his weight problem, such as a thyroid condition. Even if your dog is slim and trim, it's still a smart idea to check with your vet before beginning any new puppercise regimen!

BASIC EXERCISE REQUIREMENTS BY BREED

Minimal Puppercise Requirement 

- Cavalier King Charles spaniel
- Miniature pinscher
- Pekingese
- Pug
- Toy poodle

Low Puppercise Requirement 

- Basset hound
- Beagle
- Bearded collie
- Bichon frise
- Boston terrier
- Chihuahua
- Dachshund
- English bulldog
- English toy spaniel
- French bulldog
- Greyhound
- Lhasa Apso
- Miniature poodle
- Jack Russell terrier
- Pembroke Welsh corgi
- Pomeranian
- Shih Tzu
- West Highland white terrier
- Yorkshire terrier

Medium Puppercise Requirement 

- Afghan hound
- Airedale terrier
- Alaskan malamute
- American bulldog
- Border terrier
- Borzoi
- Boxer
- Bull terrier
- Bullmastiff
- Cairn terrier
- Chow Chow
- Collie
- Dalmatian
- English cocker spaniel
- German shepherd
- Giant schnauzer
- Golden retriever
- Great Dane
- Great Pyrenees
- Irish wolfhound
- Labrador retriever
- Miniature schnauzer
- Old English sheepdog
- Pointer
- Rhodesian ridgeback
- Rottweiler
- Saint Bernard
- Standard poodle
- Standard schnauzer
- Weimaraner
- Whippet
- Wire fox terrier

Highest Puppercise Requirement  

- Australian cattle dog
- Australian shepherd
- Border collie
- Doberman pinscher
- English setter
- English springer spaniel
- Gordon setter
- Irish setter
- Newfoundland
- Shetland sheepdog
- Siberian husky

I've *heard* about people who do. In any case, the best way to keep your dog occupied is to exercise with him!

There's no "recommended daily dose" of puppercise, but your vet can give you some guidelines, and you can also read up on your dog's breed. A Yorkshire terrier will have different workout needs from a golden retriever—but *every* pooch needs exercise!

Dear Lucky

Dear Lucky,

I am a little dog. My mom carries me everywhere. She tells her friends that I am too "delicate" to walk in the wild, but I love to run. How can I help my mom realize that I want to zoom around the park, not be toted around 24/7?

Born to Run
Gary, Indiana

Dear Born to Run,

Wow, your mom sounds like she really loves you, but I can't tell you how many of my petite friends have the same gripe. In fact, Paris Hilton's pretty-in-pink Chihuahua, Tinkerbell, was just telling me the same thing the other day. Anyway, here's what you need to do. The next time she puts you down at home, dash around the house as fast as you can. If you can, jump on furniture, leap from rug to rug, and make her worry that you're going to tear up the flooring. Now, when your mom tells you to calm down, do not, and I repeat, *do not* calm down. You want her to realize you are an athlete and that you were born to run and move those little legs. If she doesn't get the picture the first go-round, keep at it. Eventually, she'll let you walk and run on your own—if only to tire you out!

Yours truly,

Lucky

Oldies but Goodies—Walking, Running, and Swimming

WALKING

My friend Max always tells me, "Wendy, you gotta walk before you can run." Usually he's referring to relationships (so of course I ignore him, because it's obvious that the best approach to take with those is to sprint as fast as Jackie Joyner-Kersee), but he's got it right when it comes to exercise. Walking your dog is free, easy, and fun.

Just because you're doing something simple like walking doesn't mean you have to walk the same old route every day. Variety is the spice of dog life too. Take mini-adventures, go hiking, check out the park by the water, or meet up with a friend in another neighborhood for a doggie date.

Lucky's Top Five Reasons to Pound the Pavement

If you other puppies are like me, you worry about your human. You spot her sneaking into the kitchen for that last piece of chocolate cake at 2:00 a.m. or eating one too many egg rolls during her weekly *Kung Fu* movie marathon. The solution? Get your mom on a leash and start steppin'. For her health (and ours), I've compiled some of the benefits of walking that'll keep your human in shape. Studies have shown that walking can

1. Strengthen your heart. Walking can reduce mortality rates among males and can reduce the risk of heart attack in women.
2. Improve brain activity. Walking at least 1.5 hours per week can improve your cognitive function.
3. Decrease depression. Walking thirty minutes three to five times a week can reduce symptoms of depression by nearly half!
4. Improve physical dysfunction. Walking can decrease the chance of having a physical disability as you age.
5. Reduce the risk of breast or colon cancer. Walking can reduce chances of breast cancer by nearly 18 percent and can potentially prevent colon cancer altogether.

Source: medicinenet.com.

The Dog Days of Summer

The warmer months of the year bring a host of outdoor activities to enjoy with your dog. But, like humans, dogs are susceptible to sunburn and skin damage. Here are a few tips on how to protect your pal during the dog days of summer.

- Apply a pet-intended sunscreen of SPF 15 or higher, though a baby sunblock will work just as well. Consult your veterinarian before application.
- Provide a well-shaded area for your dog to escape harmful UV sun rays.
- Limit the amount of time your pet is allowed outside during the peak sun hours from 10 a.m. to 4 p.m.
- Avoid shaving a pet's fur completely. Always leave a few inches for protection.
- If your dog gets a sunburn, treat him with cool, damp towels.
- Apply animal-safe aloe vera ointment to soothe sunburned skin.

Doggie First Aid

The more active you are, the more your dog is at risk of injury. If you're raising a city dog like Lucky, remember that the sidewalk can be full of hazards. Watch out for litter, broken glass, and uneven pavement that could cause your dog to sprain a leg. If you take your exercise to the great outdoors, keep one eye open for snakes, wild animals, and dangerous plants; oleander, azalea, tulips, yew, kalanchoe, cyclamen, castor bean, and sago palm are the most poisonous to animals.

Know your buddy. If you take your dog for a hike and he's not his usual bubbly self, he might have come into contact with something dangerous while you were gazing at the waterfall. If he's a heavy panter (and there is no shame in that, girl!), don't be too alarmed if he's taking a few extra breaths post-jaunt in the dog park. If he slows his pace and pants much more than usual, though, give him some water and time to rest. You should also have a first-aid kit on hand with sterile gloves, bandages, ointments, gauze, and the number of your twenty-four-hour emergency vet. Although we all like to think of ourselves as Dr. Dolittle, there is *no* substitute for a professional veterinarian in times of medical emergencies!

RUNNING

If you and your Dalmatian are ready to go for the gold (London 2012, here you come!) and begin a running program, go for it. But start slowly. Don't try to run a half marathon your first day out the door. Your best friend could seriously injure himself, and you're not 400-meter gold medalist LaShawn Merritt, either. To start, try a walking and running combination routine. Walk a little, jog a little, check out the cutie to the right a little.

You can also check out your local running club. Many clubs accept furry members, and this is a great way to meet other exercise enthusiasts. Or, if you prefer to take the solo route, there are millions of training programs available in books or online.

SWIMMING

Once I went to visit my friend Millie, who lives in the beautiful, untouched wilderness with four one-hundred-pound rescue dogs. Millie woke me up early every morning and the first order of business (pre-coffee, mind you; I honestly don't know how she does it) was to sprint to the nearby pond for the pooches to take a dip. She threw a ball or stick in the water and the dogs would race to fetch it. They would bring it to Millie who would repeat the process.

For an hour and a half.

They had the same routine at lunch.

And at dinner.

Now that I think about it, I can't really remember why I'm still friends with her.

Cesar Millan on Aggression and Exercise

The Dog Whisperer's training guru, Cesar Millan, warns parents about the direct link between lack of exercise and canine aggression. Hear what Millan had to say about the two when I talked to him: "The reason dogs develop aggression is lack of exercise and lack of leadership. It's not that they don't get affection. They don't get exercise and discipline. Animals are supposed to walk every day, migrate every day. It doesn't matter if you live in a huge mansion in Hollywood. The dog doesn't see it that way. They just know they are behind gates. Powerful breeds, such as Rottweilers, pit bulls, and German shepherds, if you don't give them anything to do, are going to get tense and release this frustration. When dog parents come to me, 90 percent of the time, I put my rollerblades on and I let them run. An hour later, you can notice the difference. The dog finally feels good."

Here are some tips to get you and your dog off to a swimming start. First, find a clean body of water—no doggie paddling in the Hudson, please—and approach it with your dog. If your dog seems interested, try leading him up to the water and encouraging him to get his feet wet. If he's not crazy about the idea, chances are he isn't going to be into full immersion. Give him some time and lots of praise during this process. If he turns out to be interested in H_2O, try throwing a floatable toy into the water to encourage him to give the ol' doggie paddle a try. Make sure to keep an eye out for jellyfish and broken bottles.

Anything You Can Bark, I Can Bark Better: Flyball and Agility

Perhaps walking, running, and swimming just aren't cutting it for you and your dog. There are other types of doggie exercise out there that you can both enjoy. Lucky and I must warn you, though, these two activities are not for the faint of heart. They are for energetic, athletic, and well-trained dogs (that goes for their humans, too).

FLYBALL

Flyball is a sport in which teams of dogs race against one another from the starting line, over a line of hurdles, to a box that releases a tennis ball to be caught when the dogs press the spring-loaded pad—and then back to their handlers while carrying the ball. Check out the North American Flyball Association's (NAFA) website (flyball.org) to find a local team and learn more about this fast-paced sport.

AGILITY

Let's say that running in straight lines and jumping hurdles isn't your dog's thing. If you like obstacle courses, agility could be just right. There are all sorts of different obstacle courses, and the hallmark is that the human leads the dog through the obstacle course (sorry, parents, no cheering from the sidelines in this sport). Whoever makes it the fastest with the fewest mistakes wins. Agility is open to any breed, too, purebred or mixed, so there's really no excuse not to participate. The American Kennel Club can help you find a local team and even has a rundown of events in your area (akc.org/events/agility/index.cfm).

Doggie Personal Flotation Devices

If you take your pup on a boat, invest in a canine personal flotation device. Even if he loves to swim, you need to protect him in the event of an accident. A PFD will help keep him afloat during an emergency.

Dear Lucky

Dear Lucky,

I just won my first agility competition, and I had the time of my life! I am trying to get my human to understand that I want to do this again—a lot. How can I let her know?

Winner
Des Moines, Iowa

Dear Winner,

First of all, congratulations on your big win! Wendy and I love agility . . . well, watching it at least. Which dog are you? Are you single? Anyway, on to your question. The thing to do is to remind your human of your love for agility even when she's not working on it with you. Do a back flip on the way to your water bowl or pirouette before you let the leash come on. Enough of that sort of thing and it'll be crystal clear. Good luck.

Yours truly,

Lucky

Adventures in Twenty-First-Century Pet Exercise

DOGA

Believe it or not, puppies practice yoga instinctively. Dogs—and animals in general—stretch their bodies naturally and can actually guide you through some serious sun salutations. Haven't you ever heard of the downward dog pose? Looks like Spike stretching after he wakes up from a nap! Note: leotard optional for pooch.

DOGGIE SURFING

Before you get ready to hang ten with your buddy, make sure he likes water (see swimming section). Then try getting him to stand on a board on dry land. Next, move to the water. Put him on the board and let him get used to the new sensation. He might be more comfortable lying down on the board at first.

Now, if you think you could no sooner teach your best friend to surf yourself than become the queen of England or invent a

time travel machine, there are professional dog surfing coaches. And yes, they offer classes for humans, too!

SKATEBOARDING

I don't recommend trying skateboarding at home unless you're with a canine skateboarding professional, but I do hear from all of the skateboarding dog parents that I have met—you can find most of them on YouTube, and of course skateboarder Rob Dyrdek's pup is a skateboarding *pro*—that once your dog learns to skate, he will never want to stop. Lucky says skateboards are far too déclassé for her, but with the help of a retractable leash and a harness some dogs will never step away.

DOGGIE BOOT CAMP

If you can find a doggie boot camp, they'll lead your dog through ruff workouts and obedience training for hours at a time. If there is no organized boot camp class in your area, you can create your own. Play exercise fetch—while your dog is retrieving, you are doing push-ups, sit-ups, or squats, unless the cute guy from the Laundromat happens to be there, in which case you flirt with him.

DOGGIE DAY CARE

Doggie day-care facilities are popping up all over the country, providing dogs a safe place to play and romp while you slug it out in your cubicle from nine to five. (I know—so not fair, right?) Be sure that you pick a day-care center that requires current vaccines, performs a temperament test to make sure each pet guest is prepared to play well with others, and keeps the facility über-clean. Ask your vet or fellow dog parents for recommendations.

Health Nuts: Introduction to Doggie Health

There are some tried and true ways to keep your tried and true dog healthy. First and foremost is his diet. After all, your dog is what your dog eats.

DOG CHOW LOW-DOWN

Okay, so you've got this puppercise thing down pat. Now it's time to assess your dog's diet. The first thing to consider in a dog food is the ingredients. Avoid products that list the first ingredient as grains or corn—these serve as filler and have little nutritional value. Make sure that your dog is eating quality protein (egg, beef, fish, milk, soybean). Some dog-food companies use animal byproducts not fit for human or animal consumption (intestines, feet, and even bones)—ew! You want to make sure that your dog is chowing down on quality foods that you'd be willing to eat yourself. As a rule of thumb, the more expensive the food, the better it will be (and not a single dog food company paid me a cent to say that!). The good news, though, is that you generally have to feed dogs less of the pricier food because it is packed with the good stuff and devoid of fillers.

If you switch to a new dog food and your dog seems more tired than usual, has an irri-

tated or flaky coat, is licking his paws or legs excessively, or has any other unusual symptom, consult your vet immediately. The vet can perform allergy tests to help you determine if your dog does, in fact, have an allergy. Then you can become a dog food label guru and pick the product that will keep your pet safe. My friend Luke's Labrador retriever, Teddy, had tummy troubles after every feeding. Turns out, poor Teddy was lactose-intolerant and a simple change in food made him one happy dog.

DEVELOPING A SPECIAL DIET FOR YOUR BREED

It's no shock that all dogs behave differently. So why are they eating the same? Dog food makers have known for a while that high-energy dogs have different dietary needs from low-energy dogs, that older dogs have different dietary needs from younger dogs, and that hardy dogs have different dietary needs from sensitive dogs. But recently some companies, after a study of specific breed characteristics, behaviors, and health, have begun making foods tailored to the needs of individual breeds, addressing issues such as luster of coat, propensity to obesity, and sensitive stomachs.

You can also match your dog's blood type (or region where he originated from) to his diet. First suggested by Kate Solisti in *Animal Wellness* magazine, the diet is based on the fact that dogs once survived off these regional foods by picking up scraps. The regional animal diet suggests that if you're a German breed such as a German shepherd, boxer, or Doberman—do as the Germans do and feed your pet beef, lamb, and steamed cabbage. Coastal breeds such as Labradors, retrievers, and poodles enjoy the coastal diets of fish, chicken, and duck. Research your best

The Benefits of Going Green

A recent trend growing in popularity is the organic craze, and now it's affecting your dog in a good way. By simply feeding your dog organic food, you're looking at major potential changes in his lifestyle. Let's look at some of the benefits of going organic.

- Increased energy
- Maintenance of healthy weight
- Increased health and stronger immune system
- An overall better quality of life and increased life span (very good for you!)
- Fewer problems with digestion and allergies

friend's homeland and regional diet and you may be shocked to see some amazing health results.

Consider changing or rotating the food you feed your furry sidekick every once in a while. You wouldn't want to eat the same thing for breakfast, lunch, and dinner every day for your entire life—and neither does your pup. Changing foods from a chicken-based food to a lamb-based food and back, for example, over the course of six months or a year will keep your dog from developing allergies or nutritional deficiencies.

GIVE A DOG A BONE—TO TREAT OR NOT TO TREAT

I am the first to admit that Lucky is, in a word, spoiled. Well, actually, very spoiled, but that's two words. Lucky often gets a dawglicious treat, usually when I have a nighttime snack myself. Try for snacks that are more than just yummy indulgences. Some treats are packed with special supplements to improve joints and prevent stiffness. Other treats are chock-full of vitamins, while still others function like doggie toothbrushes. Some, of course, are just yummy indulgences. An even healthier alternative is vegetables. Try carrots; they're healthier than store-bought treats and dogs go crazy for the taste.

Now, a word about table scraps. I know this isn't going to be popular with dogs reading this book (and if your dog is reading this book, I think you might have something really special going on!), but table scraps are no-nos. They teach your dog the cardinal sin of dog behavior—begging. There is nothing like a Saint Bernard begging at the dinner table to make your dinner guests bolt for the door before dessert. But even if your guests are your boyfriend's friend you hate and his girlfriend you hate even more, resist the temptation to get rid of them as soon as possible. If you give him table scraps, your brilliant dog is going to continue to beg for food at the table forever based on your one moment of weakness. Furthermore, common ingredients like salt and gravy, which make food delicious to humans, can give dogs an upset stomach or make them gain weight. And besides, this way you get the last piece yourself!

Pooch Training and Treats

Food is a great motivator. If you are working on obedience training with your dog, treats are your friend. Use liver treats, pieces of cheese, or other small tasty tidbits to help motivate your dog through sit, stay, down, and all the obedience favorites. Just remember to use small treats so you don't overfeed. Yummy treats and lots of verbal praise can usually help your dog become the best-behaved dog on the block!

Toxic and Dangerous Foods for Dogs

Bones from fish, poultry, or other animals can cause obstructions or tears in digestive tract.

Chocolate can affect the heart and nervous system.

Fat trimmings can cause pancreatitis.

Grapes and raisins can damage kidneys.

Macadamia nuts can affect digestive tract, nervous system, and muscle.

Mushrooms can affect multiple systems and can cause death.

Onions and garlic can damage red blood cells and cause anemia.

Persimmons can cause intestinal blockages or irritation.

Potatoes can affect the digestive, urinary, and nervous systems.

Rhubarb (including leaves) can affect the digestive, urinary, and nervous systems.

Tomatoes (including leaves) can affect the digestive, urinary, and nervous systems.

Any sugary food can lead to diabetes.

VEGGIE DOGS—A VEGETARIAN DIET AND YOUR DOG

Depending on whom you ask, feeding your dog an exclusively vegetarian diet might be the way to go. Not only is it good for the environment, but it can help prevent cancer and other health problems. Lucky loves her lamb and rice blend gourmet dinner, but that's not to say it's for everyone. There are multiple brands of vegetarian dog foods on the market, or you can whip up vegetarian meals in your own kitchen. My pal Zac cooks his dachshund, Heidi, three square meals a day that include things like cauliflower, whole grains, sunflower oil, apples, carrots, Marmite, and lots of other wholesome goodies. Now, that's definitely a commitment of time and energy you could be using to watch reality television, but if you are considering a vegetarian diet, you will need to do lots of research and planning—and above all, talk to your vet—to make sure that your furry friend gets all of the essential nutrients. Don't give your dog raw broccoli, Brussels sprouts, beans, turnips, or cabbage, as they cause intestinal gas, which believe me you want to avoid. Sambal, onions, peppers, tomatoes, spinach, and cucumbers are also to be avoided in dog food as they are not easily digestible.

We've included some simple recipes in this section to help get you started. Lucky has

From the Desk of Lucky Diamond

Dearest Human,

Please don't let all this talk about dangerous foods keep you from sharing delicious treats with your dog. A diet of nothing but dog food and dog biscuits is not for us. We need a little surprise every once in a while. The only humans who eat the same thing day in and day out are on Hollywood detox diets, and they all look so miserable I'm surprised you can even consider doing the same thing to us.

If you choose wisely, there's no reason you can't let your dog have a few bites with you, unless the veterinarian has given strict instructions otherwise. (I've heard from a few bulldogs on the block that this happens sometimes to chubby puppies.) Personally, I love popcorn (without much salt or butter, and only a few kernels), baby carrots, and bite-sized apple slices. I also love little hot dogs and chunks of cheddar cheese, but mom says it's not good for us to lounge around filling up on high-fat stuff. She says I can have a cheese cube or two for special occasions like holidays and my birthday, though.

Hmph.

That said, there are also some innocent-seeming foods that can be hazardous for dogs, so I must warn you. Grapes, raisins, onions, coffee, many kinds of nuts, mushrooms, alcohol, and chocolate aren't just dodgy for our bellies—they're dangerously toxic and can cause an entire array of health complexities.

In addition to the foods that are just plain poisonous, unfortunately there are lots of others that are unhealthy at best. As much as I hate to admit this—and I'm sorry to have to speak against my own interests—all high-fat table scraps should be off-limits. A little bit of lean, cooked meat is okay from time to time, but don't give us any more than a piece or two. And never, ever give us a cooked bone. Bones can splinter and cause wreckage in our digestive systems; even if we've successfully digested them in the past, you'll be tempting fate if you offer them to us again.

More and more dog parents I know are incorporating a rotating diet into their dog's regimen (especially after the 2007 food scare), alternating kibble and freshly cooked meals at chowtime. Boiled shredded chicken or hamburger meat (boiling removes most of the fat) with rice is a great homemade dog food made of people foods. And trust me, we do enjoy that home-cooked touch.

Lots of love,

Lucky

taste-tested all the recipes in this section and gives them her paw of approval.

GETTING ALL MARTHA STEWART WITH YOUR BAD SELF—COOKING FOR CANINES

I have consulted with some of my human—and canine—friends to bring you some of the best doggie recipes, and trust me: If I can cook them, you can, too. So, tie on that "Kiss the Cook" apron and get ready to delight your pet's taste buds!

Lucky's Lucky Doggie Dish

Yields 2 to 4 servings, depending on size of dog

Ingredients

- 3 pounds minced chicken meat (replace with tofu for the vegetarian dog)
- 2½ cups minced carrots and celery
- 3½ cups rice
- 6½ cups water

Directions

- Combine all ingredients in a large pot and bring to a boil.
- Reduce heat to medium and simmer until liquid is absorbed and rice is tender, about 25 minutes.
- Cool completely and serve.
- Store covered in refrigerator.

Vegetarian Wendy Diamond's Doggie Meat Loaf

Yields 12 servings

Ingredients

- 1½ pounds lean ground beef (replace with tofu for the vegetarian dog)
- 3 stalks celery, chopped
- 2 carrots, grated
- 1 apple, cored and diced
- 2 eggs
- 2 slices bread, torn into pieces
- 1 cup regular rolled oats

- 1 cup wheat germ
- 3 carrots, chopped
- 1 stalk celery, cubed

Directions

- Preheat oven to 350°F.
- Grease a large pan with oil and set aside.
- Using your hands, mix all of the ingredients together in a large bowl.
- Divide the mixture into four equal parts and shape them into loaves.
- Places the loaves in a roasting pan.
- Bake for 80 minutes, or until meat is cooked all the way through.
- Allow to cool thoroughly.

Everyone's Favorite Dog Treat

Yields 18 servings

Ingredients

- 1 tablespoon (or 1 package) dry yeast
- 3½ cups lukewarm chicken or meat broth
- 3½ cups unbleached flour
- 2 cups whole wheat flour
- 1 cup cornmeal
- ½ cup skim milk powder

Directions

- Preheat oven to 300°F.
- Dissolve the yeast in broth and set aside for 10 minutes.
- Combine the unbleached flour, whole wheat flour, cornmeal, and milk powder in a large bowl. Add the broth and mix until a dough has formed.
- Roll out dough on a flat, clean floured surface until it is ¼ inch thick.
- Cut shapes from the dough and place on greased cookie sheets.
- Bake for 45 minutes.
- Allow biscuits to harden overnight.

BUT WAIT A MINUTE . . . DO DOGS EVEN CARE ABOUT THEIR DIETS?

Let's be honest here: If it were up to Lucky when it came to eating, eventually Goodyear would be able to hire her as a blimp. The truth is, dogs don't care about what they're eating, as long as it's yummy, so it's important that you stay strong and not fall for those puppy eyes. You want to be looking in them for a lot longer, so keep the food healthy and the portions reasonable!

Choosing the Vet of Your Dog's Dreams

There are some choices in life that you want to take very seriously—like finding a spouse, deciding between living in the city or suburbs, and finding the top that goes best with your Jimmy Choos. But the perfect vet is more important than all of these. Your pooch's doctor should have all current certifications and licensure, be insured, and have lots of happy clients who are pleased to recommend him or her. The office should be conveniently located. If you have an emergency, you'll need veterinary attention immediately.

Make sure your vet has a relationship with a twenty-four-hour emergency veterinary clinic so that if your pet has a middle-of-the-night emergency, you can easily get help. Finally, you need a vet who takes the time to give your pet a thorough checkup on each visit and answer any and all questions you may have. If you visit a vet and don't hit it off, don't feel guilty about moving on. Lucky went through two vets before she found her Dr. Right, and the three of us couldn't be happier. Now, if only finding a date for Saturday night could be so easy!

WHEN SHOULD I TAKE MY PET TO THE VET?

Let's put it this way: Your dog should grace the vet's door with his furry presence at least once a year, but every six months is ideal. When your dog is a puppy, you will need to go much more frequently, for vaccinations, checkups, and so on.

Unfortunately, there are some circumstances in which you might have to take an unplanned trek to the vet. If your pet has vomiting, diarrhea, or other changes in bowel activity (color, consistency, frequency, volume, etc.), refuses food or water, or displays any other unusual symptoms for more than twelve hours, it is best to go to the vet for a checkup. And if you're not sure, you can always give your vet (or the emergency vet) a call, explain your pet's symptoms and let her decide whether he needs to get his furry behind in to see the doc! If you notice less drastic changes in your pup's personality, health, or overall appearance, better to give the vet a call and see what she thinks than just to assume everything will be fine.

Does My Vet Have the Right Credentials?

Make sure your vet graduated from a veterinary school accredited by the American Veterinary Medical Association. You also want to pick a doggie doctor who has the official DVM (doctor of veterinary medicine) after his or her name. You should look for a vet who has all of the necessary licenses in your state; check the website for the American Association of Veterinary State Boards (aavsb.org) to find out what they are. It's a good sign when your veterinarian is involved in professional organizations, attends conferences, and engages in professional learning opportunities. The vet should make his or her credentials easy to find—look for diplomas or certificates in the office, or check out the vet's biography if the clinic has a website.

Fitness Forever

See? Getting fit and staying healthy with your pet isn't impossible, and it's actually fun. Just remember that you are your pooch's best friend and that means you are his advocate. After all, you want to spend as many years of bliss as possible with your pet, and that means making sure he gets his exercise, eats healthful foods, and sees the vet regularly—especially if the doggie doc's cute.

Dog Home, Sweet Dog Home

No matter how hectic your schedule gets, how many meetings or cocktails or cabana boys you need to have before the day is done, chances are that if you take a deep breath, picture home, and exhale, you'll be a little calmer. There's a reason all Dorothy Gale had to do to get back to Kansas was think of home. Home, sweet home—it's where the heart is . . . and where your dog's heart is too.

A happy dog in residence is one of the best ways to transform a mere house into a home. Smart choices, a little training, and a few tools can keep hair, scratches, and other dog-induced messes to a minimum. With the right decorating decisions, your home can be the setting of a fairy tail—um, tale; sorry—with the yappiest of yappy endings. Here in the Big Apple, Lucky and I visit the homes of other city-dwelling dogs (and their people) and find places that are stylish, smart, and impeccably clean. New York has one of the tightest, most limiting real-estate markets in the world; unless you live in a major metropolitan city, chances are that the average Manhattan apartment is slightly smaller than your kitchen. Or maybe your bathroom. Or your bathroom closet. The point: If we New Yorkers can make pet ownership and fabulous decor work together, given the limitations we have to work with, then anyone can.

Here's how.

The Four-Paw Floor

Dogs spend most of their time with all fours on the floor, and if you're not careful with your choices, it will be difficult for canines *not* to scratch, shed, and stain the material—and be banished to the backyard, forlorn and defeated. Not only are hard surfaces easy to clean and durable, but unlike carpets, they don't trap dog hairs or odors.

Removing pet hair from solid-surface floors is a breeze—just a speedy sweep or vacuum and it's gone. I do a quick brush-over of mine once a week, living out my secret

Donna Reed fantasy, and it's more than enough to keep our home looking clean and gorgeous. It's certainly far easier than trying to wrest fur fibers away from carpet fibers, an activity about as fun as . . . as fun as . . . oh, dear. I can't thing of anything less fun than that.

Wood, tile, and laminate floors all stand up well to pretty much *anything* your dog can deliver. While wood is the aesthetic champion of the three—nothing gives a better visual foundation to a fabulous room—it's also the most vulnerable to damage. Wood floors come in countless styles and finishes; try to choose a hardwood that will be resistant to scratching from dog nails. Adding a water-based finish (especially a catalyzed water-based finish, such as that used in bowling alleys and gymnasiums) can be pricey but will probably pay for itself in the end. My friend Jane installed mahogany floors in her new house when she moved in with her two dogs, and six years later there's still not a single scratch visible to the naked eye. Friends who have moved into places with older or softer wood floors, though, have reported some scratch damage, especially from bigger dogs. Wood floors are also the least repellent when it comes to doggie mistakes; tile and laminate don't retain scent or stain mementos of doggie accidents, but wood can.

If you decide to forgo wood in favor of laminate flooring, be careful: Though laminate is lovely and virtually indestructible, it can also be very slippery for puppy paws. What feels like a normal floor to us is more like an ice rink to our dogs, without the hot chocolate or the cheering fans. Most dogs can gain confidence on a new flooring surface over time, but if your dog is skittish—or if he's older and already has to take care when walking because of hip dysplasia or arthritic joints—this is probably not the right choice for your home.

If solid flooring simply isn't possible for you, carpet definitely has its advantages. You don't have to worry about scratches, and your canine will probably have more fun than on a wood floor. Accidents can be an issue, of course, but we'll get to ways of dealing with those in a little bit.

Whether you have solid-surface floors or wall-to-wall carpet, area rugs are definitely a human's (and a dog's) best friend. Choose inexpensive rugs to complement your hard-surface floors and to offer your dog a cozier place to rest; to give him an extra cushy spring in his step and protect expensive carpeting, use area rugs over wall-to-wall carpets in areas where your dog spends the most time. A well-placed throw rug is easier to clean—and far cheaper to replace—than carpet. Be sure you put rugs over nonskid, gripping backings—you don't want your dog to turn your lovely rug into a flying carpet as he runs to greet you at the door.

Keep your furry friend's colors in mind when buying rugs and carpet. My friend Lorraine made the mistake of buying a deep red rug for the living room she shares with her adorable tan-and-white corgi, Lucy. Lorraine

Patterns That Go Well with Dog Hair

Patterns can hide dog hairs more easily than a solid color. Consider a racy stripe, a nubby tweed, or a paisley print; each of these designs will make dog hair practically invisible.

spent way too much time vacuuming light Lucy hairs off the red rug, until she decided it was either the rug or Lucy. Of course she picked Lucy with no hesitation, but why force yourself to make the choice at all?

When it comes to choosing materials, rugs made from sisal are durable and easy to spot clean; nylon is also a soft and cleanable carpet option. Wool and frieze work well, too, but stay away from berber (dog's nails get stuck in the loops) and pile (it'll show paw and nail prints too easily). For carpets without the risk of long-term stains, consider carpet tiles—you get a soft surface underfoot, but individual tiles can be replaced whenever you need. They're like wee-wee pads, but far more chic.

Safe Coats, Dog and Otherwise

When dealing with choosing a wall color home owners should never forget about their pint-sized housemates. The only force stronger than a child's desire to write on walls is a dog's desire to lick them. Avoid using paints with high levels of volatile organic compounds (VOCs), which, being carcinogenic, are harmful for both you and your dogs. A better alternative is to use eco-friendly paints with low amounts of VOCs or, even better, paints made from all-natural ingredients with no VOC at all, like clay paint, composed of earth-based minerals, or lime wash, made from a combination of calcium-based minerals and water.

Fabulous Furniture and Fabrics

Okay, so you just bought that new piece of antique furniture you've been eyeing for the past few months. But the instant it's in your house, your dog starts eyeing it, too. So how do you and your dog reach a compromise and keep your furniture looking like the day you bought it?

In my house, it was an easy decision to let Lucky share the couches, the chairs, and even the bed. She's usually bathed and groomed, she doesn't shed, she's smaller than a tote bag, and she doesn't need to mark her territory with her scent—she knows the apartment is already hers. And I've certainly had furrier things in my bed any number of times. (Mind out of the gutter, please. I grew up with big dogs.)

If your dog is a generous shedder, if he's big enough to take up more than one couch cushion, or if he's got a Napoleon

Dear Lucky

Dear Lucky,

I'm a frisky mutt, and I like to take long walks and run no matter what weather conditions are outdoors: sleet, rain, snow. The only problem is my paws and coat get soaking wet sometimes and I am getting the impression that it irritates my mom when I run in the house and get mud everywhere. What's a dog to do?

Frisky
Boston, Massachusetts

Dear Frisky,

First of all, remember it's good to be the dog that you are, no matter how dirty you get. Either explain to your mom that you need to have a place where you can dry off before entering the main house—like a doggie mudroom or area, complete with a paw-drying towel rack and monogrammed foot towels—or that you need to get some doggie boots to keep your paws dry. If you've been out in the city snow, make sure your mom gets all the deicing salt off your paws; otherwise, it could hurt your pads. Keep on running with the hounds!

Yours truly,

Lucky

complex that kicks in when he finds himself on the furniture, there's nothing wrong with making a dogs-on-the-floor house rule and sticking to it. You can make your dog more than comfortable with a doggie bed or a few floor pillows in places where he'll be happy to hang around—shoot for one in every room where you spend most of *your* precious time.

If you decide, though, like I did, that couches, chairs, chaises longues, and bar stools don't have to be dog-free zones, then you can absolutely allow your dog on the furniture without sacrificing its cleanliness or quality. If you follow these helpful tips regarding furniture, you'll be able to give your dog the freedom to share your space unconditionally, and he'll be deeply grateful.

- Choose smooth fabrics, which are durable and easy to clean.
- Pick tightly woven fabrics, such as twills, denims, sateens, and poplins, that provide resistance against scratches and tears.
- Microfiber, microsuede, and ultrasuede fabrics are a dog owner's best friend; they're stain-, soil-, water-, and odor-resistant but still look like fabulous designer goods. These materials come in every color of the rainbow and are completely, 100 percent doggie mess cleanable.
- Not in the market for any new furniture? Not a problem. Just keep dog-friendliness in mind while choosing a few well-placed (and washable) throws.
- Slipcovers are another great, washable option for keeping furniture pristine and pet hospitable.

If pet hair on your furniture becomes a problem, your local pet store will have rollers, sprays, and other products that will help eliminate pet hair on any surface. Or simply throw an antistatic sheet in the dryer with your hair-covered fabrics, and they'll come out as smooth as the day they were manufactured.

When Accidents Happen

When accidents happen—and if you're a dog parent, you know that accidents *always* happen—don't think that you have to call 1-800-MOLLY-MAIDS the minute you discover a problem. There are several ways for you to clean up a pet disaster using what you have at home. If you encounter a puddle on a carpet and it's still wet, place newspaper on top of the stain (and below it, if possible). Apply direct pressure by standing on top of the stain and repeat until the puddle is all dried up. *Voilà.* Now simply rinse the remaining area with cold water. If the stain is on a rug small enough to go in the laundry, and add a pound of baking soda to the wash and regular detergent. You'll smell and see the difference.

When these household tricks don't do the job, there are countless products out there that guarantee they will. Any high-quality pet stain and odor neutralizer will do the trick, but if odors and stains are still embedded in your carpet or furniture, try renting a wet-vac from a local hardware store. If you get a strong enough machine, it'll even pull some of those ancient hairs out from the depths of the carpet fibers, and you can get a head start on knitting your Christmas sweaters.

If you're the proud owner of one of the top five drooling dogs (basset hound, bloodhound, bullmastiff, Saint Bernard, and boxer), then you know all about the smudges and marks he leaves on various parts of your house and your car. It's not your precious dog's fault; the incessant drooling is caused by the fact that the skin around his mouth and jaws is very loose, which allows the drool to seep out. So if you're not cool with the

drool, pick up some drool cleaner—yes, such a product is actually manufactured; it's called, inventively, drool cleaner—to clean up not just stuck-on drool but also nose prints on glass. Usually there's even a squeegee attached.

Looking Through the Window

Dogs love having a view to the outside world, but you have to make sure it's a safe view. Avoid letting blinds, drapes, and anything with tassels or long cords hang freely from the windows; they may look attractive, but your dog will see them as play toys—and he could get tangled, choked, or hurt in the cords.

Another major danger to consider is windows that are simply open, with or without screens. No one knows your dog better than you do, so you probably know whether he's the type to jump through a window to head for greener pastures. If you've got a rambunctious dog, keep windows closed enough to prevent a flying leap to freedom. Better yet, you can upgrade to pet-proof window screens. They're affordable, very tough, and available in most hardware stores.

Someone's in the Kitchen with Your Dog

There's one room in every home where even the best-behaved dogs show their true canine ancestry: the kitchen. The smell of food, the proximity of food, the food in the garbage, that tidbit of food you just might drop at any moment on the floor—it's enough to drive a canine into a frenzy. Even Lucky, for all her doggie dignity, turns into a shameless scavenger in the kitchen. My neighbor John's Labrador retriever gulped down four chicken breasts off the countertop in five minutes while John answered the phone. (When he got back to the kitchen he saw that he'd been beat and gave up and ordered pizza, which his retriever then also ate after climbing on top of the table.) When my friend Jeanine's daughter showed up for the school bake sale,

Petpourri?

Pet stores have started carrying aromatherapy reed diffusers for dogs, to give them something respectable to sniff, rather than who knows what from the street that's been who knows where. Though she enjoys scents like jasmine, lemon, and grass, Lucky tells me she's holding out until there's a bacon cheeseburger scent; it makes sense, since that's a smell that helps most of us find inner peace and tranquility. Be careful with the stronger scents from human stores—our friends with sensitive noses can be bothered by heavy or overbearing odors. This applies to your signature perfume, too.

she had two dozen sugar cookies fewer than she'd said she would; her German shepherd had been having a particularly hungry morning.

The reason the kitchen brings out the bad-mannered and undisciplined side of our dogs is simple: You can give your dog a silver bowl, a very comfortable dog bed, and the joys of regular outings at the dog park, but at the end of the day he's still got thousands of years' worth of survival instinct in his blood. Dogs haven't been around so long by waiting patiently for food to come to them; they've hunted and scavenged and eaten whatever they could find to survive.

Sharing a kitchen with your dog requires a little extra knowledge about what dogs can and cannot safely ingest, how to make sure your furry friend doesn't tangle with any of your appliances or utensils, and—assuming you ever want to eat in peace—a stricter set of rules for the kitchen. Lucky and I are more than happy to share our guidelines for keeping the scrap cruising (and garbage digging, lunch thieving, and even run-of-the-mill begging) to a minimum.

Dog Safety Comes First

The biggest dangers your dog can find in the kitchen are of course the edible ones, and there are several that you might not even consider on the menu. I know it sounds ridiculous when someone tells you dogs have sensitive stomachs—after all, we've all heard of dogs that have eaten everything from lightbulbs to small throw rugs and simply wanted to keep playing. Let's just say, though, that for every dog who can scarf down a pair of stinky socks or a Barbie doll and live to bark the tale, there's another who will end up in the veterinary emergency room if he treats himself to so much as a single Hershey's Kiss.

Veterinarians will tell you the most common "dietary indiscretions" they see are the result of simple overindulgence and human mistakes; too often we let dogs consume foods that are too rich or treats that are downright toxic for their digestive systems. If you have a big dog, you may have found this happens when your dog helps himself to the contents of the trash can or the leftovers off the table. For smaller dogs like Lucky, it's often us well-meaning owners who are to blame, by sharing too much people food. But Lucky does have her feisty moments, especially when a piece of her favorite leftover—green pepper and mushroom pizza—is in the trash; this is when she finds super-puppy strength and knocks over the can to get that savory slice. The bionic left paw certainly helps, but it's still a marvel to watch.

To keep your dog's buffet mentality in check, invest in a kitchen trash can that's impossible for him to open. There's a whole industry of smart inventors who work day and night to come up with gadgets to protect our dogs and keep them out of cupboards and trash cans and even away from the hot surface of the stove. (All right, technically they do that last one to protect babies and

toddlers, but dogs are so much better than children; they'll never accidentally tell your friend what you said about her last night, and you don't have to pay to send them to college.) Visit the infant and toddler section of any department store and you'll find childproof latches that can be attached to cupboards and trash cans to keep out even the brainiest of dogs.

Your kitchen, what with all the gadgets, the heat and fire from the stove (in case your dog decides to jump for it), and the sharp objects, poses more physical hazards for a dog on the hunt than any other part of your home. I'm always careful to keep an eye on Lucky's whereabouts while I'm opening the oven or the fridge. Both of these places are mysterious and tempting to dogs—all those great smells—but the door is always closed. Well, Pandora was once confronted with the same kind of temptation, and look what happened to her. If your dog is the type to charge in whenever there's a great scent coming from the kitchen, be sure he's out of range when you open the oven. And if your canine is a greyhound or other professional sprinter, a gate to close off the kitchen entranceway while you're cooking is a must. If he's tall enough to reach a stovetop, invest in a range guard to keep his paws (and searching snout) out of harm's way.

While everyone knows to keep sharp objects out of reach, it's easy to forget about the ones you put in the trash can. Sadly, dogs

Training Tip

Got minor aggression issues with your dog? Like Dog A who thinks he's the boss of Dog B? Or one who'd really like to believe he's one rung above the kids on the family ladder? Rank in the family may never cross your mind, but most dogs feel it's something they need to know.

One of the simplest ways to remind a dog of his place gently and consistently is to make sure he knows his spot in the dinner line. My friend John has two dogs and three kids. His younger, smaller dog used to try to assert himself over the older, bigger dog and sometimes even over the kids. In response, John set up the family dining schedule like this: First the family eats while both dogs wait and watch (no begging allowed). When the people are finished, the kids feed the elderly retriever while the scrappy little guy waits and watches some more. Last, after he sits on command, the pipsqueak enjoys his dinner. This one simple adjustment in the family's routine has made a huge difference in the behavior of this little dog. No one ever had to raise a voice or offer a punishment. Instead, the whole family pitched in to help their dog learn that, loved though he is, he needs to keep to his place in the household pecking order.

are often injured when they try to sniff out a treasure in the trash or the recycling bin and encounter something other than food, like broken glass or the jagged edges of open cans. Luckily, this is easy to avoid. Make sure to take any sharp objects to the outside trash or trash chute immediately, and, if you don't have one already, please go buy a safety can opener right this instant. This kind of opener leaves both the lid and the can itself without any sharp edges—safer for you and your cruising canine.

Sharing the Bathroom

The dog-proofing precautions mentioned in the kitchen section apply to the bathroom as well. All prescription drugs and medicines should be locked in high cabinets (if raisins can wreak havoc with a dog's health, what do you think a bottle of aspirin would do?) Dogs, forever on the lookout for the next snack, have been known to consume everything from baby aspirin to cough drops to cold medicine—all of which can be extremely dangerous for them. And while you may secure your medicine cabinet to keep your dog from self-medicating, many dog parents offer their dogs human over-the-counter drugs when they're sick or in pain from too much running with the wolves at the dog run. The American Society for the Prevention of Cruelty to Animals (ASPCA) warns that this practice is potentially very harmful. If you think your dog would benefit from something in your own medicine chest, please stop, call the vet, and ask before you administer even a single dose of a human pharmaceutical remedy.

Hygiene products like shampoos and soap should be kept in hard-to-reach places as well. (Hard to reach for your dog, that is. Not for you. If you've been keeping your soap in a place where you can't reach it, this may not be the book you need most right now.) This includes all lotions and perfumes, which often smell pretty edible to dogs but can make them very sick if ingested. Also be sure to keep mouthwash out of reach—the boric acid is poisonous to dogs.

Keep in mind that there are other kinds of hazards, too. My friend Becky had an unsettling toilet paper unraveling problem with her dog Lox, for example, but she changed the direction of her toilet paper (from forward to backward) and Lox hasn't TPed her living room since.

Clean and Safe Canine Surroundings

No matter how gigantic or minuscule your home or apartment is, keep the clutter to a minimum and check the floor often. A seemingly harmless small object on your floor could cause a world of problems for your dog, who might not be able to tell the difference between a bottle of bleach and a safe toy. According to the ASPCA, most poison cases from last year were attributed to household products.

Cleaning products can be extremely harmful and should be kept locked up and out of paw's reach at all times. In addition, be care-

ful when you use any product on your floors; keep dogs away until it dries completely. The pads on your dog's feet can be very sensitive to chemicals, and if they get itchy, then your dog will lick the chemical residue off—which can result in one very sick dog.

One particular danger to dogs comes courtesy of Mother Nature: common house and garden plants. For organisms that are essential for our survival, there are a lot of plants that can ultimately harm our dogs, and the shame is that some of them are so beautiful. The list

Safety Patrol

In addition to the foods, plants, and miscellaneous dangers listed in this chapter, the Humane Society of the United States also warns us about these worrisome objects and products:

- Tobacco: Chewing on a pack of cigarettes could easily lead to nicotine poisoning for dogs. Secondhand smoke is harmful to pooches, too.
- Electrical outlets/extension cords: Dogs are indiscriminate chewers, so be sure to cover all exposed outlets and place extension cords where little puppy teeth can't reach.
- Pennies: Ingestion of these coins can lead to zinc toxosis, which can cause an upset stomach, anemia, and even organ failure.
- Antifreeze: This product is responsible for thousands of dog fatalities every winter. Antifreeze smells sweet, so it's tempting, but it's deadly poisonous. If you must have antifreeze in your home, keep it and any other hazardous chemicals in a locked cabinet out of reach of both pets and children.
- Pesticides: Naturally, you'll lock obvious pesticides up right next to the antifreeze, but sometimes these chemicals are hidden. Amitraz, used in some dog tick collars, is poisonous if ingested. The packaging on mouse and bug baits can appear substantial enough to deter a curious dog—but sometimes it's not. Assume that any product designed to kill something is potentially harmful to your dog, too.
- Rubber bands, strings, and yarn: All of these items are easy to swallow and can cause intestinal blockages or strangulation.
- Plastic bags: A dog caught in a plastic bag—including a grocery bag, where he might search for remnants of food—can easily choke or suffocate.
- Small objects: Any nonfood object small enough for a dog to put in his mouth should be viewed as a choking hazard and kept out of reach.

of poisonous plants is a long one (which you can access online at aspca.org), but among the most dangerous are daffodils, tulips, foxgloves, and poinsettias. So do your dog diligence and check twice when picking plants to seed in your garden. Mind you, this is not a home decor suggestion to use fake plants, which do nobody, dog or human, any good.

Garden-Style Living

Lucky is a city girl, so unfortunately there's no romping to be done in a yard of our very own until we can afford that gorgeous rooftop penthouse; given New York real-estate values, that day ought to come in 2176 or so. Until then, we've got dog parks and the dog-friendly streets of New York City.

But if your house has a yard, you've got to cover your dog's safety before you can let the guard dog inside of you relax. Above all, make sure your dog isn't roaming off into the neighborhood unattended. I recommend a physical fence high enough to prevent your dog from leaping over, low enough to the ground to prevent escapes, and with enough integrity to keep intruders like skunks, raccoons, and neighborhood bully dogs from bothering your precious pooch.

For aesthetic reasons, some people aren't fans of visible fences. If you're one of them, one option is to install an electric fence. A typical system consists of a buried wire around the yard's perimeter, with a radio antenna that sends out a signal whenever your dog gets too close to the perimeter. The signal activates a battery installed in the dog's collar, emitting a prickle akin to that produced by static electricity. Although the underground fence is user-friendly and often less expensive to install than its visible counterpart, there are a few drawbacks: Underground fences won't be able to keep out animals looking to play with your unsuspecting dog, they need regular maintenance, and they could be ineffective with dogs that have high pain thresholds. Furthermore, the idea of shocking an animal (no matter how mildly) understandably makes some dogs and their parents very uneasy. I let Lucky watch *One Flew over the Cuckoo's Nest* with me a few weeks ago, and she's actually hiding under the bed while I type this paragraph.

One last word about yard safety: If you use chemicals to fertilize or to control weeds or insects, please keep your dogs away from the treated areas for at least twenty-four hours. Better yet, choose pet-friendly products for your lawn—you'll find them labeled either "pet safe" or "veterinarian certified"—so as to avoid the risk of your dog getting poisoned when exploring home turf.

Dippin' and Diggin' It

For water-loving dogs, a pool is a gift from doggie heaven. The chlorine in home swimming pools is as safe for dogs as it is for humans; just use a strong conditioner when you bathe him so his coat won't get brittle over time. While you can go the heated, inground route—and if you do, Lucky and I

Training Tip

I think we can all agree that the worst part of being a dog owner is picking up poop. If you'd like to spend less time and energy picking up in the yard and having to watch your step outside, choose one particular patch of grass and make it the official "rest area." It can be in your backyard, too, not off I-95. Training most dogs to go in just one spot is easier than you think. First, mark off the area with posts. Next, stuff the pockets of that jacket or sweater you keep by the door with a few dog treats. When it's time for your dog to go out after a meal, hook on a leash and go with him. Walk him to the special spot, and wait. If at first he doesn't do his business there, try, try again. When the big moment arrives, praise your puppy like crazy and give him a treat. Then keep at it. Quick-on-the-uptake dogs can figure out that you want them to go to the new potty area every time in just a few days. If your dog takes a little longer to learn, keep going with him on the leash and offering encouragement—before long your yard will have only one small landmine zone for you to worry about. Be aware, though, that concentrating Sparky's business in one small area will kill the grass and make it brown. I guess that's why we have sod!

No matter where you are walking your pet, whether it is through your neighborhood to a friend's house or out for a stroll on the streets of the big city, always remember to bring the tools necessary to clean up after him. It doesn't matter if you have a state-of-the-art pooper scooper or an old plastic bag from the grocery store; what matters is that your dog does not leave anything behind. Allowing him to do so increases sight and smell pollution, and nobody wants to step on a poop mine.

are well known to be *fabulous* guests at pool parties—your dog will be just as happy with a simple wading pool. A friend's Lab, Francine, used to splash around and try to get as wet as possible in her water bowl. Now that she's got a pool of her own, Francine happily passes her days dropping her tennis ball in the water, going in after it, dropping her tennis ball in again, going after it, dropping—well, you get the idea.

Finding a way to keep the digging dogs happy requires a different kind of play area. Choose a small part of the yard that's okay for digging (and separate from that new potty area); think of it as a sandbox. Mark it off so your dog can figure out that there's a boundary, and then make it entertaining for him. Partially bury a couple of his favorite toys and let him dig in. Put a treat out there from time to time and watch the dirt fly. Keep him company and cheer him on when he's digging in his special spot. Dogs love nothing more than to find that you enjoy the same things they do, because it provides a sense of

companionship. While you may not be all that excited about mucking up your yard looking for dog toys, it won't hurt you a bit to give your dog ten minutes of pretending it's the cat's meow. That, fellow dog owners, is what true doggie love is all about.

Posh Dogs: Priciest Dog Homes Ever?

Posh doghouses may cost a pretty penny, but kennels designed by world-renowned architects apparently cost a small fortune. During the 2006 unveiling of his design for a Las Vegas Alzheimer's center, Frank Gehry participated in a charity auction and received a commission for two doghouses, at the price of $350,000. Best known for his postmodernist architecture, Gehry has created some of the most heralded buildings of our time, including the Guggenheim Museum Bilbao and the Walt Disney Concert Hall. The lucky dogs on the receiving end of his commitment to charity live in Las Vegas. Good-sport Gehry admitted he was shocked at how high bidding went, then explained he'd have to meet the pooches to assess their design needs. Whatever the dogs' preferences, you can Gehry-n-tee that their new digs will be the toast of Sin City.

Go West, Young Dog . . . or East, or North, or South

My first dog was named Pepper. Whenever we tried to take Pepper out to the car, it was a major struggle, because she knew that when she got out she would be getting a checkup, a flea bath, or a shot, and none of that ever really got her tail wagging.

It's been many dog years since the days of Pepper, and boy, have things changed. It's true that every once in a while, Lucky's ultimate destination is the vet, but far more often we'll end up in St. Petersburg, Russia, Cancún, Mexico, or any one of hundreds of other pet-friendly cities around the globe. (Some cities seemed pet-unfriendly when we arrived, but by the time we left, Lucky had won them over.) Each exotic locale we've loved has taught us more about traveling together, and we'll share everything with you. In this chapter you'll find umpteen pages of names, numbers, and secret passwords we've collected over the course of our travels—everything you need to plan a vacation that you and your dog will never forget. As the creators of the pet-stigious Cesar Five Dog Bone Awards for the pet-friendliest companies around, we at Animal Fair Media have spared no effort to give you the dishy and cushy inside scoop. We make it easy to find the most pet-obliging transportation, the hippest carrying bags, the most practical accessories, the most welcoming hotels and resorts, and the most glamorous programs created especially for your dog.

Getting Ready for a Canine Adventure

Traveling with your dog is like traveling with your kids—you'll have to do a little extra planning (unless you're traveling with your dog *and* your kids, in which case the book you need is not this one but *Zen and the Art of Parenting*, though it might be a better idea to skip the books entirely and invest in a good therapist). Say you decided to take your kids to, for example, Las Vegas. You might spend a few moments ahead of time investigating possible activities that are, I don't know, not illegal in forty-eight other states. It's the same with dogs. You'll want to make sure that your hotel isn't run by Fleas "R" Us under the management of Cruella de Vil. Is it safe for your dog to fly? Are antianxiety drugs for dogs a good idea? What paperwork do you need to bring? Is your dog even ready to go on a trip? Complicated questions—but don't worry; stick with us and your travel plans will go off with, as the French say, *paw de problème.*

A Canine Collection of Carriers

The first step before going *anywhere* with your dog is finding the right dog carrier,

The Go-To Checklist Before You're Off

Just like humans need passports and immunization records, there are a few things every dog needs before traveling. Consult your veterinarian to confirm that it's safe for your dog to travel, and make sure your pet has all of the following before any major trip:

- Have a picture of your dog around at all times (like you don't already!). If your dog is, God forbid, lost or stolen, the photo can help prove ownership. Dogs have been known to be stolen from airports, so be extra careful.
- Have proof readily available that Sparky has had his shots and is rabies-free. Your dog must have a current health certificate, certificate of acclimation, and rabies certificate, all available from your vet.
- Make sure your dog's license is current. It should be renewed January 1 of every year unless a lifetime license is obtained. A license is the only legal protection your dog has should it get picked up by authorities!
- The essential carry-on no matter how you choose to set off on your adventure is the microchip. This is a tiny capsule the vet injects under a flap of skin on your dog's neck; the injection hurts your best friend less than getting his nails clipped at the groomers.
- Try to keep your furry companion away from the dog dish before a major voyage. I know it sounds difficult (especially with those puppy-dog eyes looking up at you!), but feeding your dog six hours before the big trip makes it more likely he'll get sick.
- Raindrops on roses, whiskers on kittens, bright copper kettles, and—well, maybe not the kittens. But make sure you're packing all of your dog's favorite treats, toys, and blankets. Small reminders of home will make a world of difference when you and your pet are a world away!

and that can be about as complicated as buying what Lucky calls a human carrier—you know, the thing with the ignition and wheels.

The premier airline-approved pet carrier was created by Gayle Martz, a former airline attendant whose inspiration was her Lhasa Apso, Sherpa. Realizing how unsettling it would be to travel without her pet by her side, she began thinking of ways he could come along, and so the Sherpa Bag was born. The ultimate in pet comfort, style, and safety, it's now the officially approved in-cabin carrier for several airlines. Fortunately, countless entrepreneurs have followed in Gayle's footsteps, and now there's a carrier for every dog at every price. In addition to affordability, though, there are some other principles to keep in mind.

KEEP IT LIGHT!

Dog bags come in different sizes with different strap lengths to suit each pet parent's comfort level. For dog's sake, remember you want a lightweight bag, to add as little weight as possible to *your* precious cargo. As my friend Jillian's pug got heavier and heavier, her back ached more and more, but when she tossed her heavy bag in favor of a light one, her back troubles went away.

ADJUSTABLE STRAP

Lucky isn't very big, so I carry her around in a carrier bag that hangs from my shoulder on an eighteen-inch strap. If your strap is adjustable, you can wear the bag in the traditional single shoulder carry—what I call the "working girl"—or you can sling it around your opposite shoulder and wear the strap sideways across your chest.

POCKETS, POCKETS, PAW-CKETS!

When I got Lucky I gave up on purses, so all her carriers have to have ample pockets. My favorite one holds my lipstick, my keys, my chewing gum—and Lucky herself, of course.

COMFORT

Dog carriers are essential, because they keep your cuddly canine safe in a secure environment. Just remember to ask yourself, does the carrier you're considering give your pet enough room to wiggle around, and is it padded for your canine's ultimate comfort? Is the dog carrier well ventilated? Will it fit in the proper place on the plane, train, or taxi? If not, you'll be hearing about it the whole way there—and so will everybody else!

AFFORDABILITY

Local pet chains such as PETCO and PetSmart carry affordable, reliable brands that you and your dog can trust. Designers such as Coach and Louis Vuitton offer some of the most sought after bags in Hollywoof—some go for thousands of dollars, but sometimes you can find one on eBay for a lot less than they cost on the shelf. Who knows—you might even be buying one of Paris or Britney's old dog bags!

Dear Lucky

Dear Lucky,

We used to travel more by car, and oh, boy, did I love to stick my little head out the window and taste that open air. But now that Mom and Dad are doing a lot more travel via the friendly skies, I get cramped and claustrophobic sitting in a tiny carrier for four hours at a time. How do I let my parents know they need to "let the dog out of the bag" sometimes?

Cramped
Closter, New Jersey

Dear Cramped,

Unfortunately, most airlines don't allow dogs out of their carriers during flights, so it's really important to be comfortable in yours. I tend not to advocate unruly behavior, especially while traveling by plane, but if your mom and dad have given you a carrier without enough room, or proper ventilation, or adequate water, there should be a price to pay. Bark like hell until they pay attention and make you more comfortable flying. And when the flight attendant gives you that cold stare because you are disturbing the other passengers—keep barking. Your owner will fix everything for you real fast and I am almost positive that you'll get airline peanuts out of it too!

Yours truly,

Lucky

Packing for Your Pooch

Lost toys, misplaced doggie snacks, and an extra-thirsty pet can happen at any time, so keep the stress level to a hair minimum by packing ahead for any situation. Always bring your pet's own food and snacks that you know he'll like. And don't forget the bottled water—dogs need to remain hydrated at all times. Lucky insists on purified water, but I think she's a little spoiled—dogs can drink regular water, just like people. Bring an extra leash and collar for rest stop areas, city tours, pet parks, dog runs, beaches, and hotel lobbies. A dog tag is also a must. Your dog's name, address, and telephone number should all be legibly written on it, and as you head out the front door, make sure the tag is on his collar, where it should be.

Up, Up, and Away!

If you're taking an airplane trip, you want to do everything you can to make the flight as stress-free for your dog as possible. Make sure your dog is familiar with the pet carrier or crate he's about to spend a substantial amount of time in. If a direct flight (always recommended) isn't possible, try to get a long layover in order to give you time to walk him. Speaking of which—arrive at the airport well before you would if you were traveling petless. Once you've checked in, take your dog outside so he can relieve himself and have one last walk before taking to the pet-friendly skies.

Cargo Dog-o (Crate Travel)

If your furry friend will be traveling in the cargo hold, make sure the crate has plenty of ventilation, secure door latches, and a comfortable cushion for the little (or big) canine voyager. When labeling your crate, use a sticker that is not easily removed. For extra staying power you can cover it with clear mailing tape. Use a dark permanent marker to write your name, address, telephone number, and final destination, as well as your canine's name and age and the time of his last feeding. When your pet is traveling in the cargo hold, the maximum combined weight of the dog and crate should not exceed one hundred pounds.

Tell the flight attendants at the beginning of the flight that you have a dog in the cargo hold, and remind them a few times during the flight, so the captain can monitor the temperature and air pressure while you're in the air. The temperature in cargo holds is not moderated when planes are on the ground, so if you're flying in the summer, try to book an early morning or an evening flight; if in the winter, a daytime flight. Take nonstop flights whenever possible—considering how often airlines lose baggage, you *really* don't want to risk your dog.

Cargo flying can be traumatizing for dogs, so make sure you get yours used to being in the crate when it's moving (walk around with it in your house while reassuring your furry friend in a soothing voice). You can even consider making a tape of airplane noises so he won't be surprised when the engines start to roar.

Mile-High Club: Lap Dogs

When taking off to the friendly skies, in-cabin travel may be an option for smaller dogs. Label your carrier exactly the same way you would a travel crate. Also, always check the airline's rules and regulations for in-cabin pet travel. Every airline has size restrictions on pet carriers, so make sure yours is an appropriate size. You can find the rules and regulations on the airline's website before embarking. Pack a few of your furry flier's chew toys and some yummy treats in the carrier, to help him keep quiet during the flight, but keep in mind that a squeaky toy is probably not the best thing to take on a plane—at least not as far as the other passengers are concerned!

Nausea

If your dog is anxious about the trip, there are many natural herbal options to calm him down, available in your local pet store or natural foods store; if he's a particularly nervous flier, you can get a prescription for something like clomipramine (aka "puppy Prozac"), but be careful, as oversedation is the leading cause of animal deaths during airline transport. And, of course, it's vital that you consult your vet before making any decisions regarding antianxiety medications.

Frequent-Flier Miles for Two

We have all heard of frequent-flier miles but some pet-savvy airlines offer pet travel programs, where frequent-flier miles and awards are issued when you travel the world with your pet. Here's a look at some of our favorites, but the specifics of the programs may have changed in between when I wrote this and when you're reading it, so no matter what airline you fly, go to petflight.com to find out about its pet benefits and requirements before you commit to a ticket.

One airline that encourages a trip with man's—and woman's—best friend is MIDWEST AIRLINES (midwestairlines.com). Their Premier Pet Program allows you to use Midwest Miles (fifteen thousand to twenty thousand) to pay for your pet's travel either below cabin or in-cabin.

Each time you use JETBLUE's (Jetblue .com) JetPaws service you will be issued two True Blue points; get enough of them, and they'll add up to a free flight. JetPaws also holds contests like the PET LOOK-ALIKE Contest where you can submit photos of the two of you for a chance to win an exotic vacation. JetBlue won *Animal Fair*'s Cesar Five Dog Bone Favorite Airline Award last year—and it was well deserved!

Lucky and I usually fly with CONTINENTAL AIRLINES (continental.com), which has also won the Cesar Five Dog Bone Award, twice. Continental flies animals as cargo rather than as checked baggage—which, given how often airlines can lose luggage, is a *very* good thing. We dog parents can track our little doggie loved ones online at Continental's cargo website, cocargo.com, as we fly. Continental also accepts small pets for in-cabin travel on certain flights. PetPass members can earn frequent-flier miles when transporting a pet using their PetSafe service. Sounds like a win-win situation—four paws up, Continental.

DELTA AIRLINES (delta.com) also has a great reputation when it comes to traveling with all sorts of animals, though unfortunately you'll have to keep all primates and reptiles as cargo. You can even fly with two pets in the main cabin. But if you think dealing with two dogs on an airplane is hectic, take a direct flight to Argentina and see the world-famous dog walkers toting twenty pooches at a time. Bow-WOW!

EL AL Israel Airlines (elal.co.il) was the first international airline to offer in-flight pet perks, in 2001. After three trips in a three-year period your continent-hopping sidekick can earn a free ticket!

With its Passport for Pets program, Virgin Atlantic Airlines (virgin-atlantic.com) is leading the pack in international travel, and with good reason. On your dog's very first flight on Virgin Atlantic he's given a welcome-aboard pet pack that includes a toy mouse and a Virgin collar tag. But that's not all; he also gets a passport that records his flights and allows him to collect "paw prints" redeemable for gifts like handmade Virgin bowls or for donations to his favorite registered animal charity. Or, if you've been a dog-gone great parent, your doggie can choose to donate one thousand bonus air miles to your Virgin flying club account.

Paw-blic Transportation (Trains . . . and Buses)

When it comes to public transportation, your dog can board the bus or subway with you as long as he rides in a carrier that fits on your lap. (Sorry, big dogs, but you'll have to stick to the streets unless you've got special guide- or assistant-dog privileges.) If your travel mode of choice is the train, go online to animalfair.com, where you can find specific guidelines for your own local rails. Amtrak has a strict no-pet policy, so don't even try to give those puppy-dog eyes to that hunky train conductor, thinking you'll be able to get on board—if you want your dog to travel with you, your only hope may be to sneak him aboard. Unfortunately, all commercial bus companies have similar no-pet policies—including, if you can believe it, the curiously named Greyhound.

Pet Travel Advisory

Do not put your dog on a plane to any of the following places.

Australia	Barbados	St. Lucia	Antigua
Japan	Jamaica	St. Vincent	Hawaii

Pet quarantines in these destinations make traveling there hairy and unpaw-pular. If your furry friend wants to see these locales, he'll just have to wait for the YouTube clip.

If you're vacationing in Europe, your pet is free to travel on almost all trains in France, Germany, and Italy; on the United Kingdom's National Rail, dogs are always welcome and small dogs even travel free. Larger dogs' ticket prices are half the fare of a standard adult ticket, and usually the dog must be crated up and wear a muzzle. I think it's time Amtrak starts learning a thing or two from the Europeans and includes pets when announcing, "*All* aboard."

Also, going out for a night on the town with your canine sidekick can be a fur-tastic time; just make sure that when you hail that taxi you are settled and seated before your dog jumps out of the bag and gives you away. New York City's Pet Taxi is a unique kind of cab service because it will drive your tail-wagging treasure anywhere "with or without you!" Pet Taxi's services extend to pet shipping, from SoHo to Singapore; this may seem as odd as shipping your great-aunt Louise across the Atlantic, but Pet Taxi works with the U.S. Department of Agriculture, so they know their stuff.

And as for boats—well, ferries tend to allow pets on the exterior decks as long as they are well behaved and leashed. And of course your dog is both!

The Great American Road Trip (Automobiles)

I love road trips. Driving with Lucky makes me feel like I'm Thelma and she's Louise. Or is she Thelma and I'm Louise? Who knows, but the resemblance ends when it comes to driving off a cliff. Not really our style. We would, on the other hand, wear head scarves and hang out with Brad Pitt. Traveling by car with your furry sidekick is by far the top way to go—what dog doesn't like sniffing the wind with his snout out the open car window? You can relax and take your time, see some touristy sights like Mount Rushmore or the Shoe Tree in Nevada (here Lucky can chew on as many shoes as she wants—except mine) and drive down some of the most scenic roads in the United States, like the Pacific Coast Highway in California, the Bayou Byways in Louisiana, the Rocky Mountain Ramble in Colorado, and Skyline Drive in Virginia. And all these vacations can be low-cost and fun.

Rest areas can offer more than just physical relief from the road. When cruising the pavement with your pal try to choose rest areas that have lots of grass and space away from the parking lot and other people. Sometimes these rest stops aren't so easy to find and you may have to create your own. My friend Dave was driving in Alaska with his German shepherd, Nate, when they realized they both had to go and there wasn't a rest stop for miles. Dave pulled over on the Seward Highway, letting Nate do his business at the same time he did. While they don't recommend making such an audacious pit stop if it can be avoided, Dave and Nate did remark that they got to see some caribou (and caribou droppings) from a unique vantage point.

Try to stop every two to three hours so your pet can stretch his legs and get some

Before You Hit the Open Road

Just like flying, you will need to do a little extra planning before heading off with your dog in the car.

• Plan accommodations in advance! It would be terrible to be turned away at a roadside motel because of your furry sidekick—especially after a long day of driving. In a perfect world all lodging areas would accept pets, but luckily, in this one, AAA publishes "Accommodations Offering Facilities for Your Pet" in a set of four regional directories.

• Give your pet flea and tick treatment. The places where you're traveling to may host parasites that are not indigenous to your home, so exercise caution by applying treatment before the trip.

• Pack ample food and treats as well as water for your pet. Cars get hot and dogs get thirsty, especially when they're spending half the trip with their head out the window.

• Be sure to stick to your dog's regular eating schedule. You will need something to serve your pooch his food and water. Find a two-in-one portable dog food and water bowl set (two separate compartments unzip to hold both food and water, as well as some of your dog's favorite treats); your local pet store will carry this, as well as other pet travel gear such as a water bottle that unfolds into a bowl. Or if you're feeling homemade, just bring along some old Tupperware with lids so the food and water can be locked up and spill-free on those curvy roads.

• Toys are invaluable on a road trip. A toy is a great way to tire out your dog on a pit stop so he can stretch his legs (all four of them).

• A dog bed or old blanket will be nice to offer your pet if your car isn't as cozy as your couch at home. The bed or blanket will also help prevent your dog from sleeping on your lap, which is dangerous and illegal; if you're caught, you'll get a hefty fine.

• Leashes, leashes, *leashes*! Leashes are extremely important on any road trip. You will need to keep a tight hold on your adventurous pet in foreign surroundings.

exercise or leave a territorial marking; always offer him water at the *beginning* of your break to prevent the water from making an uninvited comeback all over the center console once you get moving again. A rest area is also the pet perfect spot to throw away your pet's empty snack packages and water bottles and to situate your dog's toys and food bowls for the next furry leg of your journey. Go to petswelcome.com to find out which rest stops on your route might be particularly dog-friendly.

Helping Carsick Dogs

Let's face it: Not all dogs are accustomed to long car rides—or car rides at all, for that matter—and some may get "canine carsick." All dogs are different, but here are a few tips to prevent your dog from getting sick on the open road.

- If you keep your dog on the floor of the car, away from the windows and unable to see outside, he should avoid getting sick at all.
- Some dogs need to see the direction they're going. If this is the case, move your dog to the front seat so he can pilot with you, know the direction ahead, and avoid dizziness from the backseat.
- Sometimes if you just distract your dog with a bone or toy to chew on, he won't even notice the bumpy ride.
- Your dog's behavior may have to do with static from your car seats. To prevent any static interruptions, put a small rubber mat on the floor and the car will be shock-free.
- Ask your vet about using ginger or other remedies that will settle your dog's stomach. Some vets suggest giving your dog motion sickness medications like Dramamine, but be absolutely sure to consult your own vet first.

The Right Car for the Right Dog

Companies like Toyota, Volvo, and Jeep have all begun to make furry-friendly cars, including things like rear-hatch pet ramps, doggie booster seats, pet seat covers, and more! Check PETCO and other pet stores for these items.

Dog Seat Covers—If your dog is a shedder and you don't have leather seats, you are going to end up with one hairy ride. Seat covers are an easy way to keep your car in decent condition without banishing your dog to the floor.

Dog Seat Belts—If your car isn't equipped with a pet seat-belt system, install one! A dog seat belt is always a good idea on busy main roads and expressways, especially when you're unfamiliar with the traffic.

Dog Car Seats—A dog seat is another product you might want to consider for a long road trip. Some companies have begun to expand into car kennels and even dog hammocks! A seat or bed made especially for him will keep your dog safe and comfortable.

Lucky's Tips

I've journeyed by car, plane, subway, plane, bicycle, and taxi. Let's face it: I'm one of the most well-traveled dogs in the entire country.

One of the most important things to remember when traveling with humans is that they are calling the shots and, in some cases, taking them, too. Remember you are their pet (or so they think—wink-wink, woof-woof) and you will probably have to acquiesce to their itinerary. Learn to relax, go with the flow, and always try to position yourself close to a window in a moving vehicle for the scenic view (and a slightly open window for fresh air). And don't forget your owner is on vacation as well and will be even more attentive and open to your comfort level than usual. So if you've been stuck in the car for five hours driving through the Rocky Mountains and it's time for a little relief, express yourself. Bark, whine, or scratch on the car seat. Trust me, it won't be long before you and your two-legged friend will be pulling over and taking a nature hike; she probably needs a little break from the constant driving anyway and just needed you to remind her—silly humans!

Canine Cruises

I first heard about canine cruises when my girlfriend Jennifer showed up to a Yappy Hour with her Pomeranian, Missy, whose hair was braided with beads. Five minutes later, after my laughter at the sight had subsided, I asked her where Missy had gotten her new do. Turns out the pair had gone on a cruise together, something I had never even thought about doing with little Lucky, so we immediately booked a vacation. Fortunately, it was the same month I was going through a heavy breakup, so I felt the trip was absolutely necessary. I don't know what was more memorable about that trip—the number of piña coladas I had or Lucky's sheer excitement in having her hair blow freely from the open air in the middle of the ocean. I guess that beats a dirt road.

Cunard Cruises has some of the most famous ocean liners in the world and is home to one of the most pet-friendly cruise ships, the *Queen Mary 2.* There's a growing trend of pet travelers joining the seafarers on *QM2*, especially with the woof-tastic enhancements offered by its Pets on Deck program. Sea dogs receive a complimentary gift pack featuring a *QM2*-logoed coat to keep warm in those chilly sea breezes, a Frisbee, name tag, food dish and scoop, a complimentary portrait with their owners, a crossing certificate, and a paw-sonalized cruise card. More pet perks include extra comfy beds in two sizes (Lucky needs to stretch and roll when she snoozes, so she loves the extralarge bed), healthy gourmet cookies at turndown, fleece blankets, an assortment of toys, and a selection of premium doggie food from top brands. A Kennel Master aboard takes care of the daily responsibilities such as feeding and walking, so you can relax and enjoy one more plate at the buffet or cocktail on deck before bedtime. To choose a destination your salty dog will beg for, sail over to cunard.com and book a cruise you and your dog won't soon forget.

If you're looking for something a bit smaller, a few charter companies that allow dogs are the Fun Zone Boat Company and the Red & White Fleet in California, Coopertown Airboat Tours and Scenic Cruises in Florida, and Airboat Adventures LLC in Louisiana (petsonthego.com). There's never been a better time to set sail with your dog!

Accommodations

Of course, some dogs—just like some humans—may prefer the stability of dry land, Luckily there are many hotels, attractions, and social areas that are more than happy to welcome landlubbers and their pets!

A WORD ON HOTEL PETIQUETTE

Understanding simple hotel petiquette is an easy way to make sure you and your canine companion will remain welcome at pet-friendly establishments. Keep your dog on a tight leash at all times when walking through the hotel and on outdoor hotel grounds, even if it's just a short trip to the ice machine. A familiar crate filled with your dog's favorite chew toys can keep your pet quiet and safe and prevent accidents in your room. Also, bringing your own DOG IN ROOM sign is a great way to let hotel staff know that you have a pet in your room who might not take kindly to unannounced visitors. Upon check-in, most pet-friendly hotels hand out brochures that highlight dog parks and dog-friendly restaurants; some even have special dog menus incorporated in their room-service selection. And often, even if there's no brochure, the concierge can tell you about all the dog-tastic activities to enjoy.

NO DOGS ALLOWED?

Did you know that at the Westminster Kennel Club Dog Show no dogs are allowed in the audience? It's sad but true: There are many places where people don't understand that adding a dog means adding more fun. Luckily, many hotels around the world offer pet-sitting services that will allow you to see all those no-pet sites while your dog spends the afternoon being pampered. If you're staying with family, make sure to bring a gift for the people who will be home taking care of your little furry baby while you're out!

THE UNITED STATES

No matter what the season, spring, summer, fall, or winter, Lucky knows where to venture and, most important, where to put all four paws up. Although not quite the lover of cold weather (she begs me almost daily to move from New York City to Miami or LA), she never minds cozying up with me in front of a roaring fire at a wintry destination. You'll never have to travel without your canine best friend when there are so many hotels that offer amazing pet amenities for you and your dog.

Affordable hotel chains such as BEST WESTERN (bestwestern.com) and HOLIDAY INN (holidayinn.com) all have hundreds of pet-friendly locations. MOTEL 6 (motel6.com), "America's original pet-friendly hotel chain," is another trustworthy branch that will always have a place for you and your pet to stay no matter what budget you're on. The affordable and always accommodating RAMADA INN (ramada.com) has many pet-friendly branches to put you and your four-legger up. WYNDHAM HOTELS (wyndham.com) offer packages such as the Paws and Claws promotion, which include treats to welcome your dog, food and water bowls, a comfy dog bed, free lint rollers and pet-waste bags, and a five-dollar donation per night to Greyhound Pets of America. Note: Though these chains welcome dogs, it's still a good idea to call ahead to confirm that your four-legged friend will be welcome at your particular destination.

A great alternative to hotels is to stay in private vacation rentals. Instead of a cramped hotel room, you can relax in a privately owned home with more space, often at a lower cost. Vacation rentals have added bonuses that hotels don't, such as kitchen facilities and personal and convenience items to make your stay more comfortable—just make sure the home owner knows that your dog is accompanying you. Your dog will love staying in an actual house with a backyard. Check out vrbo.com for a list of private vacation rentals all across the world.

Of course, if you're in the mood to splurge, you can consider luxury options as well. Offered in fourteen locations in the United States and even two in Canada, LOEWS HOTELS' (loewshotels.com) Loews Loves Pets program makes it impossible not to bring your pet along for the ride. All pets receive their own gifts, including a pet tag, bowl, and a special treat to kick off their vacation. Loews also has a special room-service menu just for dogs and provides a map of local dog walking routes. Dog beds, leashes, collars, videos, and rawhide bones are also available. Depending on the location, you might even be able to sign your dog up for surfing lessons!

Another great luxury hotel chain to consider is W HOTELS (whotels.com). With pet-serving hotels in almost every major city in the United States, W Hotels offer such unparalleled pet service and amenities, you would swear that this is a luxury hotel designed specifically for "the furry ones" instead of people. Upon arrival, your dog gets a welcome packet filled with a pet toy, a pet treat, W Hotels pet tag, cleanup bags, and a welcome letter with information about special pet services available through the concierge. In your gorgeous room you'll find a custom W pet bed (just as comfortable as, if not more comfortable than, your own bed), food and water bowls with a floor mat, PET IN

ROOM door sign, and a special turndown treat. Services that can be arranged by the concierge include dog sitting, dog walking, pet first-aid kits, grooming, and locations of the nearest dog parks and dog runs, as well as a birthday cake if your trip was a surprise for your dog on his annual big day.

U.S. Destinations

If you and your pooch don't have a destination in mind in the beautiful, bountiful, and pet-friendly USA, here are some outstanding pet-friendly hotels and attractions Lucky and I have discovered that are guaranteed to make your pooch feel like royalty. Listed by city, these destinations represent only a fraction of the places we've visited, so make sure you visit animalfair.com to stay up-to-date with our journeys—you can even watch our travel vlogs and see where your paws can take you. Almost all the hotels listed offer some sort of pet-welcome package that includes things like complimentary treats, hotel-logo chew toys, dog room service, food and water bowls, a dog bed, and more.

ASPEN, CO

The Little Nell Ski Resort in Aspen provides services that will give your dog an all-natural Rocky Mountain high. The Puppy Jet Lag Kit includes personal brass ID tags, a cozy dog bed, and a map of dog-friendly hiking trails; the resort also provides dog walking on request, so you can check out the skiing on each of the four mountains in the area—when you're not checking out the ski hunks, that is. To check out all this resort has to offer, click on thelittlenell.com.

AUSTIN, TX

Have you heard the phrase "everything is bigger in Texas"? Well, y'all, at the Driskill Hotel in Austin, it's true. With the Driskill's Pampered Pet program, your canine cowboy or cowgirl will receive designer dishes and a designer mat, bottled spring water, a custom Driskill pet bed, a souvenir toy, gourmet pet treats from 1886 Café & Bakery, a supply of "Doggie Business Bags" made from recycled plastic, and Driskill logo leashes and collars for those long walks through scenic downtown Austin. If this sounds like it suits you to a tee, go to driskillhotel.com to strike it rich with information.

BACHELOR GULCH, CO

The Ritz-Carlton (ritzcarlton.com) at Bachelor Gulch in Colorado is a great pet destination—and if you don't have your own dog with you, you can just borrow one when you get there! Bachelor, the hotel's resident yellow Labrador, is a rescue dog who was found in Denver, alone and afraid. The Loan-a-Lab program allows guests to borrow Bachelor—alone and afraid no longer—for a hike or snowshoeing adventure on the Loan-a-Lab trail. The program is so popular that Bachelor is often booked months in advance. Along with the Lab himself, guests participating in the program get a Loan-a-Lab starter pack, which has a fanny pack, bottle of water, brochure about the Bachelor program, trail map, selection of healthy treats, and waste disposal bag. Humans, meanwhile, can relax in the hotel's twenty-one-thousand-foot spa. Guests are also encouraged to make a donation to the Eagle Valley Humane Society; these can be put in Bachelor's Lockbox, located in the lobby.

CHICAGO, IL

Chicago's Burnham Hotel offers the Pets in the City package, which includes not only bowls, toys, and treats, but also a copy of a pet massage book, in case you want to work out all the kinks and cramps in your dog's travel-weary body. If you'd rather get than give a massage, the Burnham can set up a limousine to take you and your dog to a local spa. They also donate five dollars of the proceeds from each reservation to PAWS (Pets Are Worth Saving) Chicago, a nonprofit organization working to build a no-kill city in which homeless dogs and cats find loving homes. Check out this luxurious and generous hotel at burnhamhotel.com.

Or try the James Hotel in downtown Chicago (jameshotels.com), steps away from Michigan Avenue, which means major shopping for you and your dog. The hotel features a David Burke restaurant that not only serves delicious human food but also offers delicious meals for dogs, including steak tartare, gourmet doggie bagels, real bones, and an after-dinner doggie-safe mint. If you're looking for a day trip you can enjoy with your dog, you're not too far from Navy Pier and Historic Buckingham Fountain, which allows leashed dogs to join the fun.

LOS ANGELES, CA

Los Angeles offers some of the most pet-friendly hotels in the country, like the fabulous Hotel Palomar (hotelpalomar-lawestwood.com)—dogs *everywhere*—or the pet- and budget-friendly Residence Inn by Marriott (marriott.com), but one of its best pet-friendly attractions is Runyon Canyon Dog Park. Runyon Canyon is a 160-acre park, and more than half of it allows off-leash puppercise and amusement. You and your pup might get a tad starstruck at this regular stomping ground for celebridogs—Lauren Conrad, Demi Moore, Ashton Kutcher, Amanda Bynes, and Orlando Bloom are just *some* of the celebrities who take their dogs to Runyon Canyon. Runyon Canyon is also home to a variety of wildlife, including birds, snakes, lizards, and coyotes, so have your guard dog up and always remember safety comes first, especially in the wilds. But once you see the view, you'll know it's all worth it.

Huntington Beach in Southern California is home to the one and only official Dog Beach. Huntington Dog Beach is a nonprofit corporation where you can donate money to keep the beach clean and open for our sun-loving, furry friends—and why wouldn't you? When it's time to stop frolicking and go to sleep, just down the road is the Hilton Waterfront Beach Resort (hilton.com), which overlooks the Pacific

Ocean and miles of white sand beaches; not only is the view incredible but you can play an invigorating round of beach volleyball while your canine enjoys a wild game of chase the seagulls.

And if you're feeling adventurous, the Loews Coronado Bay Resort outside of San Diego (loewshotels.com) can offer your pooch surfing lessons complete with a surf-and-turf dinner and an aloha collar!

MIAMI, FL

If you're looking for some Latin flavor but don't want to travel outside the country, then Rickenbacker Causeway Beach in Miami, Florida, has more than enough spice of life for both you and your dog. This beach is one massive stretch of ocean, extending the length of the Rickenbacker Causeway from Downtown Miami to Key Biscayne. Not only are dogs allowed on this entire stretch, but there are two types of beaches: a tree-lined dirt beach and a standard sandy beach, so your dog can run from sand to dirt whenever he feels like switching it up. Where to stay while in Miami is a no-barker: the Loews Miami Beach Hotel (loewshotels.com).

NANTUCKET, MA

The Woof Hotel has its own fenced-in dog park complete with benches so you can watch your little one run around and play. It also offers a "Yappy Hour" every Friday from 6:00 p.m. to 8:00 p.m. through the months of July and August; you and your saucy canine socialite can meet other guests in Woof Park to play and enjoy doggie treats and custom-made Cisco "Hair of the Dog" beer. If this sounds like the getaway you'd want to get away to, then visit harborhousevillage.com to find out more.

NAPA VALLEY, CA

Vincent Arroyo, owner and founder of Vincent Arroyo Winery in Calistoga, California, once told me, "You can't make wine without a dog." And now the term "man's best friend" is finally being taken seriously, as a plethora of Napa Valley wineries have opened their doors to our four-legged pals. In some cases dogs are allowed in the tasting rooms; in others, only on the grounds. Just remember not to let them clean up any spilled wine; drinking it can cause damage to their kidneys and, of course, slurred barking. Lucky and I have found dogs all over Napa, like Chianti, a beautiful golden retriever living at Domaine La Due at the base of beautiful Mt. George; Gypsy, a young poodle who lives at Provenance Vineyards; and Pumpkin, who resides at the Crichton Hall Vineyard—after an adventurous career as the pet of the Marketing Director of USA Wrestling, she now spends her days as "Protector of the Vines" chasing squirrels and turkeys away. And after a long, hard day of getting your paws dirty, you can curl up at any number of dog-friendly lodgings from corporate hotels like the Napa Embassy Suites to beautiful historic mansions such as the Napa Inn Bed and Breakfast (napainn.com).

NASHVILLE, TN

Everyone knows that Nashville is home to American country music, but it may soon be the home of canine country music, too. The Loews Vanderbilt in Nashville (loewshotels.com) is revolutionizing the music industry one bark at a time. At Loews Vanderbilt you and your canine singing sensation can take part in the "Hounds of Music" program, which sends you in a limo to a chic recording studio for some time to cut a track with your bandmate. The barks and notes are then mixed and mastered to create an instant classic.

After howling with your dog, you must check out one of Nashville's best kept secrets: Warner Park, a twenty-seven-hundred-acre recreational area on the west side of town that offers miles of stunning nature trails, picnic areas, and sections of paved roads where no vehicular traffic is permitted. Park Rangers at the Nature Center are also generous with doggie biscuits. Riverfront Park is another Nashville must-see; this dog-friendly zone features a reconstructed pioneer settlement depicting Nashville's earliest history and outstanding river views.

Two more pet-friendly lodging options in Nashville are the Regal Maxwell House (home of Maxwell House Coffee), and the historic Union Station, which once served as a thriving L&N Railroad passenger hub. Take a look at millenniumhotels.com and unionstationhotelnashville.com.

NEW ORLEANS, LA

Ritz-Carlton, New Orleans (ritzcarlton.com), in the historic French Quarter, is the one-stop destination for a pet ready to get fat on Fat Tuesday. The Ritz keeps up its luxe reputation when extending its Creole/Cajun hand to dogs. Just call ahead and the Ritz will have your dog's bed fluffed and ready right next to yours. While in the French Quarter, dog lovers must see the work of native painter George Rodrigue, who creates one-of-a-kind "Blue Dog" pet portraits right in the neighborhood on Royal Street.

If you're planning to be in town for Mardi Gras with your Mardi Dog, come a week early to enjoy the excitement of Barkus, the Big Easy's Mardi Gras specifically for canines. Each year a special pet-related parade theme is chosen to honor dogs in New Orleans. Past themes have included "Joan of Bark," "Lifestyles of the Bitch and Famous," "Tails from the Crypt," and "Jurassic Bark." Of course, after all the parade pavement pounding, a huge pawty follows. It's a night you and your dog cannot miss (barkus.org).

NEW YORK, NY

Known for being one of the fashion meccas of our country, Manhattan proudly barks over seven hundred licensed pet retailers in the city. Shops include Le Chien (lechiennyc.com) and Petropolis (petropolisnyc.com), where you and your shopping partner in crime will delight in fashionable doggie duds.

Retail spaces are small and crowded, so always check for a NO PETS ALLOWED sign before entering any store with your dog and respect the wishes of the store owners and managers, no matter how badly your pup wants to leave his scent at the establishment.

If you're up for some games and a nose-licking good time, then head over to trivia night at Brooklyn's Bar Great Harry, where they welcome doggies of all sizes into their one-of-a-kind establishment. When you're ready for more, go on to the Brooklyn Ale House, where upon entering with your furry pub partner you'll hear a chorus of "Welcome to the Dog House!" Other pup-friendly bars include the Levee, among whose regulars is a fancy feline named Lucinda, and the Pacific Standard, where you and your pub-crawling pal can catch a poetry or fiction reading.

Taking your canine sidekick with you out for dinner can be as easy as finding a restaurant that has an outdoor patio, or finding a headwaiter who doesn't pay attention. Remember to tie your dog's leash to your chair as opposed to the table—Lucky has knocked over many glasses of unsuspecting water, wine, and beer to get to that piece of errant chicken. Some of Lucky's favorite dining spots when she's home in New York City are Fetch Bar and Grill and the Cherry Tavern in the East Village, where peeps and pups can dine indoors under one roof. Since restaurants are not allowed to use their own glasses or dishes to serve pets, bring your own doggie bowl to hold food or water for your canine dining partner.

When it comes to resting your head, whether human or canine, you can't do better than the London NYC Hotel (thelondonnyc.com)—permanent home to Lily and Bentley, the manager's two English bulldogs—or the SoHo and Tribeca Grand Hotels (grandhospitality.com).

SAN FRANCISCO, CA

The Golden Gate Bridge is one of the architectural wonders in the U.S. of A., so when you make the trip to northern California to experience it, don't leave your dog at home. The Hilton San Francisco has just undergone an extensive forty-five-million-dollar transformation, and is the place to stay to enjoy the Dogs of the Bay package. In addition to toys, treats, and a comfy bed, the Hilton also has dog-sitting and -walking services so that you can rest and relax in the award-winning five-thousand-square-foot full-service day spa. Prepare to pamper yourself by visiting hilton.com and making reservations!

SANTA BARBARA, CA

To celebrate your puppy love, try visiting the San Ysidro Ranch, the "Most Romantic Destination in the World." It was the setting of Vivien Leigh and Sir Laurence Olivier's wedding and hosted the honeymoon of John and Jackie Kennedy. All pets are allowed on the seventeen miles of walking trails, and the ranch will even supply you with a dog to walk if you couldn't bring your own or if your pup would like a friend to come along! Need some relaxation time after a day of breathtaking sights, beautiful gardens, and exhilarating views of the Pacific? Both you and your pet can get in-house massages from the staff. For more information on the ranch, visit sanysidroranch.com.

Other pet-friendly hotels in Santa Barbara include the Doubletree resort, the Casa Del Mar Inn, the Harbor House Inn, and the Four Seasons Biltmore, all located near Santa Barbara's many parks and beaches. Stop by the Douglas Family Preserve, a leash-free park that allows social dogs to meet and greet and also boasts stunning sights for the owner. Other dog-friendly parks that welcome dogs include Chase Palm Park and Oak Park. One essential stop for the Santa Barbara dog-loving tourist is the Carivintâs Winery, home of the Dog Lovers Wine Club. Since the club's start, profits from wine sales have supported the Humane Society of the United States, the Orange County German Shepherd Rescue, and both the New Orleans and Los Angeles ASPCAs. Check out doubletree.hilton.com, hotelcasadelmar.com, harborhouseinn.com, and fourseasons.com/santabarbara.

SEATTLE, WA

The Hotel Monaco in Seattle is one top dog when entertaining pooches. Upon arrival your pet gets checked in to their VIP (very important pets, woof to that!) registry, and if you are in town for business instead of pleasure the hotel can arrange a personalized doggie itinerary to keep your barking baby happy while you're out ruling the world. To accommodate your mini-me, the hotel sells monogrammed dog coats with the Hotel Monaco Seattle logo; this is both practical and charitable as not only do you go home with an adorable souvenir, but also ten dollars from each sale is donated to the King County Humane Society. There is also a list of services for the Downtown Dog Lounge where your pet can receive a full wash and blow-dry as well as a forty-five-minute pet massage. For those times when you have to travel but can't bring along the furry-faced light of your life, Hotel Monaco offers the original Guppy Love, a complimentary companion goldfish along with fish toys so you will never have to spend the night pet-free. Sound interesting? Please visit monaco-seattle.com for more information.

STOWE, VT

Another ski vacation destination is in Stowe, Vermont, at the Topnotch Resort and Spa. After you and your furry friend have spent the day strolling on the Recreation Path, hiking trails on Mt. Mansfield, or chasing squirrels through the woods, the spa at Topnotch offers your four-legged explorer an in-room Rover Reiki Massage given by one of its specially trained therapists. If skiing is not your cup of tea, this resort offers rides through historic Vermont along wooded trails and into meadows on new elegant Victorian or surrey carriages. Mountain biking, canoeing, and fly-fishing are also available, allowing you and your pet the time and freedom to get back in touch with nature. If Vermont sounds like a place you and your dog would love to visit, go to topnotchresort.com to see everything this resort has to offer.

WASHINGTON, DC

When you go to DC for political partying, you can stay at the Fairmont, where the Pet Package includes a paw-print door hanger to keep your dog from surprising the maid. For every Pet Package, the Fairmont donates 5 percent of the room cost to the Washington Animal Rescue League. Another option is Hotel Palomar (hotelpalomar-dc.com), which boasts a stellar pet concierge who can get you information about pet playtimes, day care, grooming services, vet hotlines, and even pet massages. Also consider heading to the Doggie Style Bakery Boutique & Pet Spa for an afternoon of grooming and doggie cake (doggiestylebakery.com). If you're in town during the right season, don't miss a walk along the cherry-blossom-lined streets or a trip to Rock Creek Park.

International Destinations

Just because you're leaving the country doesn't mean you have to leave your pet behind. Countless international cities had pet-friendly reputations long before the United States even existed.

ATHENS, GREECE

Dogs have always been a part of Greek mythology. Lailaps was a dog who tried to hunt down a terrifying fox that had a reputation for being uncatchable. Because Zeus feared the mighty dog might never catch the pesky fox, he put them both in the constellations to give them all of time to resolve their battle in the heavens. But today,

Who Got Lucky

The word is out—Lucky has the hots for Jennifer Aniston's corgi-terrier mix, Norman. She met him once at the Bar at the Four Seasons Hotel in New York City. Ever since their first sniff, Lucky has been smitten. She also appreciates Jennifer Aniston's take on dogs and men; the actress has been quoted saying, "It wouldn't be bad if, when a man comes home, he'd run to his woman with his tail wagging. This sort of excitement is something I've always missed in a man, to be honest." Lucky couldn't agree more and knows that Norman has been well trained by Aniston and would make a great love catch. Besides, Norman likes to stay at the Four Seasons, an establishment famous for pampering pets like royalty, offering any size pet beds, pet food and water bowls, chew toys, cooked meals served via room service, concierge service that arranges getting favorite pet foods from outside the hotel, and dog walkers and sitters on request. Norman, if you're reading this, give Lucky a call. Seriously.

From the Desk of Lucky Diamond

When my mom travels for business and will only be gone for a day or two, there are only two doggie hotels that I will rest my paws at: Stay Hotel in Chicago (staydoghotel.com) and the Wag Hotel in Sacramento or San Francisco (waghotels.com). Stay Hotel provides all-glass suites with a dog's-eye view of the river and wildlife. I also get a comfy bed, toy chest, fresh flowers, and black and white (my favorite colors) prints by Keith Carter. Wag Hotels have the ultimate in luxury suites, and my mom always books the very best. Here I sleep on a premium bed with a Wag cam so my mom can see how much fun I'm having and a flat-panel TV to watch Animal Cops; classical music is played to help me relax and fall asleep. These hotels get a definite four paws up. And besides, staying away from Mom for only a day is a little therapeutic. Shhh. It's our secret. Every once in a while every dog needs some time alone.

Other Things to Consider When Going Abroad

Traveling abroad is thrilling and adventurous, but if you're a first-timer, it can make you a little uneasy, especially with a dog in tow. Here are some things to consider when traveling abroad with your pet.

- In places where drinking water is unsafe for humans, it probably isn't safe for dogs, either.
- Be aware of country customs and courtesies. For example, a mangy, unkempt dog in Paris is an extreme faux paw (then again, they don't pick up after their dogs there, so who knows?).
- Some countries require extra fees for picking your dog up at the airport.
- Consider the time of year you're flying. Some countries won't carry dogs as cargo during hot summer months.
- All countries in the European Union require a pet passport, which can be obtained from your vet and will help you avoid long, scary quarantines.

you don't have to look up at the stars to see dogs in Greece. Athens is known for its high dog population, made up in large part of well-fed, clean, tame street dogs. The city has started "treating" street dogs by neutering or spaying them, implanting a microchip, putting a collar on them so citizens know they're being taken care of, and releasing them back onto the streets.

Pet-friendly accommodations come in all price ranges from the Hilton to the London Hotels. With breathtaking views of the famed Acropolis and Parthenon, regal Constitution Square and the Parliament, lush Lycabettus Hill or the original Olympic Stadium, the Hotel Grande Bretagne (grandebretagne.gr) offers an unrivaled perspective of Athens' mythical history. Or just walk your dog inside, sneak up to the roof for the views, and go home to a rental apartment, hundreds of which are available very cheaply.

It is Greek custom to welcome pets at restaurants, but be courteous and ask first; don't show up unannounced with a drooling Saint Bernard.

AMSTERDAM, THE NETHERLANDS

The good news about Amsterdam is there are no quarantine laws. While abroad check out the Eewal Bed and Breakfast in Leeuwarden (bedandbreakfastleeuwarden.nl). Originally a canal side house built in 1611 where the River Ee streamed by, the B&B is now fully renovated and oozing with historical charm. Other pet-friendly hotels in the area include the NH Amsterdam Centre and the palace Hotel Noordwijk aan Zee (nh-hotels.com, noordwijkaanzee.net). The Dutch love dogs, and chances are that the Hondenschool Racima (hondenschoolracima.com) will have scheduled a group playdate or a doggie/parent trip to the beach during your stay.

BEIJING, CHINA

Beijing is ranked one of the top pet-friendly cities in all of Asia (and number one in China), but this is a relatively recent development. During the twentieth century, dog ownership was almost entirely eliminated by the Chinese Communist Party, which believed that keeping pets was a trait of the bourgeoisie. But now in major cities the rising Chinese middle class has welcomed dogs back into its families, meaning far more dog-friendly sights and attractions. If you're taking your dog to China, however, you must be very careful: There are strict laws in China that limit number of dogs per home and even the size of a dog per home. The Beijing Zhong Tang Courtyard (beijinghotel-link.cn) is a historic Chinese hotel built at the end of the Ming dynasty; it's seen the likes of some pretty famous Chinese officials dating back to the Qing Dynasty.

CANCÚN, MEXICO

Say hola to sun, surf, sand, and the incredible ME by Meliá Cancun Hotel in beautiful Mexico. ME Cancun is one of the most pet-friendly hotels south of the border, so when authentic tacos and margaritas are on your mind, be sure to invite your tail-wagging *amigo* along—but for once, don't share your margarita. A breakfast buffet for two and pet turndown service is also included in this Mexican Lap of Luxury package. Your canine will be so entertained he'll never want to bark *adiós*. Careful: Mexico, like some other tourist destinations, has a large population of stray, underfed dogs. You don't want your furry sidekick getting mixed up with their crowd, as there are some dangerous pups out there. But the country is also home to the oldest domesticated dog breed in the Americas, the Xoloitzcuintli (pronounced shollo-itz-quintlee). Log on to me-cancun .travel to book now!

LOS CABOS, MEXICO

The Las Ventanas Resort has a Pets' Luxury program, and if your dog is looking to be pampered in every sense of the word then he's barking up the right tree. At Las Ventanas your hungry playmate has his own Canine Delights menu, with entrees like the Rin Tin Tin (Lucky's favorite—shredded braised beef and steamed rice), and treats (doggie chews, rawhides, and jerky). Sometimes Lucky craves lamb and rice with a side of veggies, and at Las Ventanas the chef will lovingly prepare made-to-order dishes, which Lucky just drools over. Your fluffy friend can be walked by staff along the beach or in the flowering desert countryside while you take advantage of some alone time and maybe get a massage or two yourself. Las Ventanas also offers pet cabanas that you can use either in your suite or on the beach; your pet can have as much or as little sun time as he prefers. *¡Olé!* Go to lasventanas.com to book your pet cabana soon!

LONDON, ENGLAND

London is another European city with a history rich in dogs. The bulldog was bred in London over four hundred years ago; today, London honors its canine roots by offering scores of pet-friendly hotels such as the Sofitel St. James Hotel (sofitel.com), Four Seasons Hotel London (fourseasons.com/london), and the Landmark London Hotel (landmarklondon.co.uk).

Native Londoners love to go out to the pubs with their dogs, and the hundreds of bartenders in the London area won't even blink an eye when you two sit down. The Brown Dog Bar and Dining Room is one of those places. Its rating as one of London's six best gastro pubs by *Michelin's Eating Out Pubs Guide 2008* isn't the only reason to check this pub out, though. The Brown Dog provides snacks and water bowls all day for those of the canine persuasion, and if your pup gets tired of schmoozing, baskets are available for a short snooze. You and your pet can even have your picture taken and join the resident Jack Russell, Mr. Bojangles, in the canine kennel of fame photo gallery!

MOSCOW, RUSSIA

The Novotel Moscow Centre (novotel.com) is where you want to stay with your dog when traveling to Moscow—not only the

staff love dogs, but the food is great! Make sure to visit the Laika Dog Monument, erected in 2008 to celebrate the first living mammal to orbit the earth. Don't miss a walk in Red Square, where you can see St. Basil's Cathedral and Spasskaya Tower of the Moscow Kremlin.

PARIS, FRANCE

I've seen dogs allowed in more places in Paris (inside and outside of restaurants, the Metro, stores, etc.) than anywhere else. And the pet poo-poo problem—France doesn't have a strong tradition of picking up after its pets—has become far less problematic now that street cleaners have been employed to vacuum up doggie disasters. One of my favorite pet-loving hotels is Le Meurice. While doing renovations in the early 1900s, the workers adopted a stray greyhound hanging around the site. The greyhound became such an inspiration for the workers that the hotel staff decided to adopt the pooch, and a pair of greyhounds has been the hotel's emblem ever since. In addition to housing dogs, Le Meurice welcomed legendary painter Salvador Dalí and his two tame ocelots on more than one occasion. The grooms will happily take your dog for a walk in the Tuileries Garden if you want to dash off for a rendezvous at the top of the Eiffel Tower (where no dogs other than seeing eye dogs are allowed). For more information, go to http://lemeurice.com.

QUEBEC CITY, QUEBEC, CANADA

But you don't have to go all the way to Paris to treat your chic chien to an elegant time. Quebec City, the only remaining walled city north of Mexico, offers scenic beauty, historic sites, and small-town charm in a big city atmosphere. Make sure you go to the post office to take a look at the Golden Dog of Quebec! Check out the Fairmont Le Château Frontenac, an elegant resort built in the early nineteenth century as a place for rail passengers to stay overnight. Le Château has a visiting dog program for canines under twenty pounds and offers all the necessary services for people traveling with their pets: dog walkers certified in doggie first aid; a twenty-four-hour clinic with bilingual staff (French and English); referrals for groomers, animal photographers, and pet shops; and a pet-friendly park (fairmont.com/frontenac). If you come at the right time during Quebec's seventeen-day Winter Carnival in late January through early February, you and your dog are in for a real treat—toot your red trumpet while you wander the ice palace or cheer on your favorite in the canoe races.

Now that you know how easy and fun traveling with your four-legged sidekick can be, all that remains is for you to pick a destination and be off. So until next time, au-ruff-voir!

How to Be a Real Party Animal

How many occasions are there in a year for the average human to go to a party? Let's see: your birthday, a couple friends' birthdays, Halloween, Christmas, Passover, Yom Kippur, Thanksgiving, New Year's Eve, and the Fourth of July.

Add your own special days (like, say, Wednesday), and what you've got is some pretty heavy partying. But given that for every one of our years that goes by, a dog lives seven, your dog has a *lot* of occasions to celebrate. It's about time you gave him the opportunity to kick back, chill out, and let the good times roll!

My philosophy is that there's no party that can't include dogs, or even put dogs at the center of attention. I suppose a no-dogs-allowed party would be an exception, but if anybody has ever thrown such a party I doubt it was very festive and I'm glad I wasn't invited.

I love throwing parties for Lucky, especially because she's very ecumenical: She's equally happy celebrating Christmas, Hanukkah, Kwanzaa, and Saturnalia (the ancient Roman winter festival). She got very excited when she heard about Ramadog (Ramadan for us humans), because it meant that she'd be able to start her partying much earlier in the season, but then she found out about the fasting, and that was the end of that.

Lucky eventually infected me with her enthusiasm, and we've tried to revolutionize the dog party scene. I've thrown parties like Yappy Hour, Toys for Dogs, Howl-o-Ween Costume Party, and Paws for Style; in addition to being fabulous events, these parties have raised money for notable animal organizations like the Humane Society of New York, the Best Friends Animal Sanctuary, No More Homeless Pets in Utah, and the Katrina Pet Memorial.

So forget the old saying "Let sleeping dogs lie." Let sleeping dogs wake up and *party*!

Make It a Birthday Paw-ty or Rescue Celebration!

Every dog has his day. Lucky, of course, can't tell me when her birthday is (she's probably tried, but we haven't figured out the finer points of interspecies communication yet). Fortunately, when I rescued her I was able to get a general idea of when her birthday was. When that time of year comes around, all the neighborhood dogs come a-barking to my door, because they know what it means when I throw a birthday paw-ty: *Laissez les bons temps rouler!*

But if you can't even find out the general time of year your dog was born, fear not, because there's a day you do know that's just as worthy of celebration, if not more so: the day you brought your furry friend home. There's no reason not to have an annual rescue or adoption celebration. This is just like a birthday paw-ty—the same festive food, the same doggie decor, the same enthusiastic guests—except it celebrates the date of your dog's rescue or adoption rather than the date of his birth. Actually, even if you already celebrate your dog's birthday, why not have another celebration on his rescue day? After all, it's the day he started his new life—and the day you started yours.

So whether it's a birthday paw-ty, an adoption celebration, or a because-it's-Tuesday fest, follow these steps for a day your dog will remember for about fifteen minutes. But even after he forgets the events of the party, he'll feel the love for a long, long time.

Of course you'll make sure to have the usual decorations—balloons, streamers, and confetti. Any balloons should be placed high enough that dogs can't get to them, so your furry friend's furry friends don't think they're balls. Otherwise, your dog guests might pop them and scare themselves or, even worse, try to eat them. Emptying a few cans of tennis balls in the room will provide plenty of chewability—in the form of decorations that are both festive and safe. Festoon the room with framed photos of you and your dog. Photos celebrate both the birthday dog and your special relationship with him.

Consider a guest book for all the attendees to write birthday messages or dab their paws onto the pages. Ask your guests to record some of their favorite memories of your little one. Once the book is filled with hilarious and touching anecdotes, you'll be glad you thought to prepare such a wonderful keepsake.

Naturally, when your dog has his day you want him dressed à la mode. Now, this doesn't mean that you have to take a pup used to running around in his birthday suit and put him in a complicated, uncomfortable, um, birthday suit. It's your dog's celebration, and there's no reason to make him wear something that will annoy him. Would you want to sit at your own birthday party trying to take off your clothes because you hate them so much? Try a simple bow, a bright bandanna, or even a new collar.

When it comes to snacks, you shouldn't feed your dog and his guests traditional human birthday party food like cake and ice cream, but that doesn't mean they can't indulge. Due to the popularity of birthday paw-ties, doggie cake is on the rise and there's no longer an excuse not to have one on your pup's next big day. Find a local doggie bakery or make a dog-friendly meat loaf!

The excitement reaches its height at birthday paw-ties when it's time to play games. Dogs may not be able to play Pin-the-Tail on the Doggie, but there certainly are entertaining games that they can take part in—especially since all their closest canine friends are in attendance. A tug-of-war is a fun competition that can spin into an even more fun free-for-all. Try putting Moms and Dads up against their dogs to see who can last the longest.

Arts-and-crafts projects are always fun at a birthday party, so what would a birthday paw-ty be without paw-painting? Cover a small area of floor in newsprint and set up containers of standard, nontoxic finger paints and thick paper. Make sure to have a place for

Lucky's Party Tips

As a dog with a few birthdays under her collar (you can ask how many, but I'll never tell), I've thrown some of the greatest themed birthday celebrations in all of dog-dom. Here are some ideas for theme paw-ties.

Barky Gras: Much like a Mardi Gras, a Barky Gras has the smoky feel of New Orleans jazz, but it's a little less Cajun and a little more canine. Get your mom and dad to decorate in purple, green, and gold, and have a parade as if you were celebrating on Bourbon Street. Make doggie masks so you can run around pretending to be wolves.

From Bow to WOW Spa Party: Have your folks hire some dog groomers for the day and treat you and your pals to a day of pampering and luxury. Anybody out there ready for a paw-dicure? And hey, why not include your parents' friends, too? We aren't the only ones who deserve to be treated like kings and queens!

Doggie Paddle Party (at the beach or pool): If you have a pool, an off-leash dog beach, or lake nearby, get together with your friends to bask in the water for some real doggie-paddling fun.

Other ideas: Wild Woof-Woof West Party, Hawaiian Bow-Luau, Costume Party, Hollywoof Party, Animal Party, and '80s Doggie Disco Party.

puppies' paws to be wiped off. Not only is this fun, but it will also provide future paw-ty decorations and maybe even frameable art! Meanwhile, put a bunch of bandannas in another corner with glue, glitter, and other decorative stuff—so that parents can participate in the arts and crafts, too!

Don't leave your guests barking for more—hand out good-doggie bags full of exciting treats. A few Milk Bones and a tennis ball would be fun for four-legged guests. If you want to go the extra mile, consider coupons or gift certificates to local pet businesses. Check out a local dog groomer, doggie spa, or doggie day care and ask about multiple gift certificate discounts. You can also go the other direction and make the paw-ty a fund-raiser for a school or sports team!

Planning Your Own Mutt Makeover®

When I first rescued Lucky I had no idea what I was getting into. I knew I wanted to bring a dog into my life, and I knew I didn't want to buy a designer puppy who came groomed, primped, and pedigreed to perfection. I'm a down-to-earth Ohio girl, and I needed a down-to-earth dog. When I met Lucky, it was puppy love at first sight.

But when I got her home, I realized that she was . . . well . . . just a tiny bit *too* down to earth. The workers at the shelter had more important things to do than give its residents expensive haircuts, so I took Lucky to a salon and had them give her the works. She came out looking like she'd never spent a lonely day in her life. It was like she was Little Orphan Annie and I was Daddy Warbucks minus the Broadway musical.

But then I started thinking about all the other dogs in the shelter—the ones who hadn't found their true homes yet—and I wondered, what if some of the people who are meant to adopt these dogs come to the shelter, look around, and miss meeting their soul mate because he's a little too scrappy or had too much fun in the mud before their visit?

And so Mutt Makeover was born. We spent hours grooming a shelter full of dogs and within a week we'd lost count of how many of them had been adopted.

But why should we limit this to shelter dogs? Maybe your dog has been feeling droopy lately—a new haircut might be just the thing he needs!

And then of course Lucky pointed out the obvious, which had been staring me in the face the whole time: Turn it into a party. Throw a Mutt Makeover charity event to benefit your local adoption shelter. Pups and their parents show up needing a little style in their lives, and leave having gotten as much as they've given.

Or if you're feeling ambitious, host the event at the shelter itself and make it a combination Mutt Makeover / Open House Adoption event. People who come looking for a pet will go home with a dog groomed like a star, and everybody—human and animal—gets love and companionship in the process.

To get the dogs really clean, towels, water,

and even people are going to have to get dirty. Have enough shampoo, brushes, and towels on hand to clean the dogs and enough toys on hand to keep them occupied during the cleaning.

If you're going to provide haircuts as well as baths, have a dog grooming expert on hand. We all know what happens when an inexperienced person wields the scissors. If you explain to a professional that the party is for charity, she might volunteer her services or at least offer a volume discount.

Invite a dog trainer to give parents the rundown about the basics of doggie behavior and training—sit, stay, come, and so on. If you're throwing the event at a shelter, this can be specially helpful for new dog parents. If bringing an actual dog whisperer to the party is out of the question, how about offering some basic information, along with referrals to great trainers for the dogs who might need it?

If this is a multi–Mutt Makeover and adoption event, offer referrals to friendly local pet-related businesses your pet parents and pet guests might want to check out—you might even be able to arrange a small discount.

Dog Look-Alike Party

You know how people are always saying that some puppy parents look just like their dogs? Well, why not have a party with a look-alike contest to find out which dog and parents are best suited for each other? Ask a few pet care experts (vets, groomers, etc.) to serve as judges. First prize could be a free grooming—for the pooch and the parent.

You're going to need some sort of stage for the pooches and their human parents to strut their stuff. It doesn't have to be fancy—you can mark out a catwalk in your living room or even a local park. Set up chairs directly in front of the stage for the judges; they need to have a good view so that the best dog (and parent) wins.

Of course the main activity for this party is the doggie pageant. As the host, you can serve as the emcee and announce each dog–parent pair as they come up. Have them go onto the stage one pair at a time and tell the judges the dog's name and breed and the owner's name. After all the pairs have had a chance to impress the judges, it's time to vote. I recommend having three judges so that you don't have to worry about a tie-breaker activity.

Have a photographer take shots of each dog–parent pair. After the party, you can post them online or send a photo to each of the guests with a note thanking them for coming.

Planning Your Own Bark Mitzvah

I'm something of a mutt myself, at least religiously speaking. My mother and her relatives are all Methodist, but my father's family is from a Jewish shtetl in Russia. I've always embraced both sides of myself, and so I thought Lucky ought to be able to do the same. I never had a bat mitzvah, so when

Lucky was coming up on age two—age fourteen for dogs—I realized I didn't want her to miss out.

But I had to act fast. Thirteen is the traditional age at which humans become bar or bat mitzvah (literally, "son/daughter of the commandments"), and my JAP (Jewish American pooch) was already older than that. But I knew Lucky was heading toward a turning point in her life. Her development was age appropriate, she never barked out of turn, she was fully house-trained, she was able to spend more and more time alone, and though she still quarreled occasionally with her brother Pasha, she'd gotten much calmer.

In short, she was ready for her bark mitzvah.

So I invited all her canine friends—from all different religious backgrounds—decorated our home, got together some tasty kosher treats, and even helped Lucky study her Torah portion. The party was a smashing success, and dogs and humans alike danced the hora until the sun went down.

When your puppy turns two, why not help him make the transition into a responsible, happy, and meaningful doghood? A bark mitzvah lets a dog show that underneath his mischievous and frisky fur is the mature, loyal friend he was born to be, and the party will leave the pooches barking *mazel tov.*

Try setting up an area with a pleasant, canine-comfortable background where you can have a photo shoot. Have guests pose with their dogs or your dog (or both!) so the memories can last a lifetime.

Make sure you have some music on hand. Dancing is an essential part of any bark mitzvah, and "Hava Nagila" will inspire your dog and his guests to throw caution to the wind and dance the night away.

Horah-Fetch could be a fun way to get the dogs riled up at the party. I suggest you play this outside, or at least far away from the fine china. Find as many balls and toys as you can and start throwing while klezmer music plays. The energy of the music will fill the dogs, and they'll celebrate like there's no tomorrow!

Host Your Own Toys for Dogs Event

The first year I had Lucky, a few months into winter I noticed a big change. She finished all her food without a single attempt to send it back to the chef, she stopped having accidents in the house, she started holding her tongue around strangers even when she knew they were wrong (which was most of the time), and she seemed to forget that there was such a thing as biting.

Then I realized what was going on. It was two weeks before Christmas, and Lucky wanted to make sure that Santa Paws knew she had been nice rather than naughty. To reward Lucky for her self-control, and to make Christmas a little merrier for shelter dogs whose parents hadn't found them yet, I decided to throw a Toys for Dogs party.

It turns out that Christmas Day at the Humane Society of New York is exactly like any other day at the Humane Society of New York. No doggie stockings. No Milk

Bones and cookies. No gifts to rip open with paws trembling in excited anticipation. So Lucky and I invited our nearest and dearest friends (of both the two-legged and the four-legged varieties) to join us in their Christmas best to celebrate. Guests brought toys for needy animals so that even the rescue dogs would have something to rip open on Christmas morning. So why don't you host a Toys for Dogs event at your own home, benefiting your local animal shelter?

Two colors that won't disappoint for a Toys for Dogs Christmas festivity are, obviously, Christmas staples: red and green. Just make sure your greens don't look like grass and your reds don't look like fire hydrants. You're throwing a party, not a nightmare before Christmas celebration.

And what's a Christmas party without a Christmas tree? Decorate your tree with fun and festive dog-themed ornaments. When you hang the stockings by the window with care, don't forget to include one for your pet. Pooches love digging into stockings with their noses to sniff around for treats.

You'll also need a beautiful display basket for the donated toys. Make it flashy and big so that guests who forget to bring a toy will turn around in shame, drive to the nearest pet store, and come back with two. Make sure to keep the basket on a table or somewhere else above canine reach—you don't want the dogs at your party turning the gift toys into used gift toys.

Hire a Santa to make sure all the guests have a jolly time. Have your favorite uncle, goofy brother, or plump neighbor play Santa and sit for a jolly photo shoot with all the four-legged guests. Make sure dogs get their photos taken whether they've been naughty or nice!

Dogs love music, so adapt popular tunes into pet-oriented songs. "Rudolph, the Red-Nosed Reindog" is one of my favorites, along with "We Wish You a Furry Christmas." Dogs and their owners will love howling out the revised lyrics.

Don't forget to serve Christmas cookies. Serve traditional cookies to the human guests, and use the recipe below and some traditional Christmas cookie cutters to make peanut butter cookie treats for the dogs.

Wendy and Lucky Diamond's Perfectly Easy Peanut Butter Treats

Yields 12 servings

Ingredients

- 2 cups whole wheat flour
- 1 teaspoon cinnamon
- 1 tablespoon baking powder
- 1 cup peanut butter (chunky or smooth, depending on your dog's taste)
- 1 cup milk

Directions

- Preheat your oven to 400° F. Grease a cookie sheet and set aside.
- In a large bowl, mix together the flour, cinnamon, and baking powder. In a sepa-

rate bowl, mix together the peanut butter and milk, taking time to do it; it can be a sticky process. Add the peanut butter–milk mixture to the dry ingredients, and mix until well combined.

- Place the dough on a lightly floured surface (away from the dogs) and knead. Roll the dough flat to about a quarter of an inch.
- Use a cookie cutter to cut out different shapes. (Lucky likes dog bones or princess crowns.)
- Place cutouts on a greased cookie sheet and bake your treats for 20 minutes, or until they're a delectable, golden retriever light brown.
- Cool the treats before serving. (Nothing's worse than an angry dog with a burned tongue.)

Enjoy!

Host Your Own Yappy Hour® Fund-raiser

When I broke up with my boyfriend in 2002, to celebrate my new freedom I threw a Yappy Hour and invited my single girlfriends, their single guy friends, and everybody's dogs over for puptails. Conversation with potential new boyfriends is easy when there's a dog to talk about, and guests donated what they could to the humane society.

The party was a mad success. The singles mingled, the dogs played, and the humane society made some dough. And thus Yappy Hour, the first ever puptail party event, was born. Eventually Lucky and I went on a trip hosting Yappy Hours across the country and raised more than two hundred thousand dollars for local charities. From Nashville to Cancún to New Orleans and back, Yappy

There are a few Christmas paw-ty don'ts that you should take very seriously:

DON'T hang mistletoe; it is poisonous to your furry guests. Other holiday plants to stay away from include holly and poinsettia. Hang a safe treat for your dog and catnip in a pouch for your cat.

DON'T leave lit candles unattended unless they are completely out of reach of your largest canine guest.

DON'T leave wrapping paper on the floor. The dogs will have a terrific time playing with it, yes, but you will not have a terrific time cleaning it up.

Hours are still helping the underdog. Why don't you join us? Follow these simple instructions and who knows—you could discover puppy love or meet your soul mate, whether two-legged or four-legged.

Start with canine-themed invitations that bark fun and excitement. Be sure to mark on the invitation that it is a fund-raiser. Choose a local charity that needs support (like your local shelter or humane society) and mark on the invite what guests can bring: dog food, checks, toys, checks, treats, checks . . .

To get your guests (two- and four-legged) in the mood to party, blast your favorite tunes on your iPod or make a mix CD filled with canine-friendly songs like "Who Let the Dogs Out?" and "How Much Is That Doggy in the Window?" to get the party howling! Maybe even play some Snoop-Dog if all your guests are of age (or if you're absolutely sure you can trust those who aren't not to squeal).

Serve human guests the appetizers and drinks you'd serve at any happy hour, but make sure you have some special doggie treats on hand, too. Canines don't have to feel left out of the martini craze! Try their very own yappetizer treats in colorful martini glass–shaped ceramic bowls. The Dog Lovers Wine Club in Santa Barbara makes delicious Napa Valley wine for humans and donates a portion of its proceeds to help local dog shelters. Each bottle of wine features an artistic doggy design that makes for a memorable keepsake. Check out dogloverswineclub.com.

Also out of Napa Valley is Happy Tail Ale, the first-ever beer for dogs! The beer is nonalcoholic and noncarbonated but made in a real brewery with artesian water and malted barley. It's brewed in authentic copper kettles and features all-natural beef drippings with no byproducts or chemicals. Unlike human beer, this beer is fortified with glucosamine and vitamin E to keep your dog healthy and happy. Check out beerfordogs.com for more information.

Important: If you're going to do a lot of drinking, don't let your dog drive! I mean, if your dog is going to do a lot of driving, don't drink. No, I mean, if your drink is going to do a lot of dogging, don't let your drive do. Wait . . . can somebody get me another martini?

Don't drink and drive, and especially don't drink and drive with a dog.

Host Your Own Howl-o-Ween

For most parents, their dogs are already princesses, angels, and goblins all wrapped into one, but during Halloween, your dog can be anything or anyone he wants to be (or anything *you* want him to be).

Halloween is one of Lucky's favorite holidays, not only for the excessive eating and trick-or-treats but also for the fabulous annual party we throw! The Howl-o-Ween Pet Costume Contest helps raise money for the Humane Society of New York and gives canines a chance to compete and show off their stunning (and more often than not hysterical) costumes.

You and your pooch can host a Howl-o-Ween charity drive for the local rescue shelter. Think of how hard you'll laugh when the neighbor's bulldog comes as Mr. T, or your co-worker's boxer arrives dressed as a scuba diver. Avoid letting your dog go as Toto, though, unless you *like* wearing Dorothy's pigtails and sparkly ruby slippers.

Nothing says Howl-o-Ween like scary, spooky decorations; just make sure they're not so enticing your pets want to eat them. Change your place from hairy to scary by hanging plush Chihuahuas dressed as bats from the ceiling. Drape cobwebs up high where dogs can't reach. Don't forget the spiders! A simple HAPPY HOWL-O-WEEN banner picturing a wolf howling at the moon might get your guests excited or a BARK OR TREAT! poster if you're in a more comic mood.

Finally, place haunting cauldrons around the room and fill them with delicious treats for humans and pets. (Keep the treats separate. You don't want to end up with a Milk Bone while your pup chows down on Skittles!) When it comes to candy, skip the chocolate. Even if it's just for the two-legged guests, you know how lightning-fast dogs can be when delicious human food falls on the floor, and chocolate is poison for dogs. But one thing your dog *can* enjoy on Halloween is the delicious taste of pumpkin. It's full of vitamins and nutrition; it's great for the coat and digestive system; and it's a recommended ingredient in weight loss and raw-food diets. Avoid canned pumpkin pie mix, though, because of the added sugar and spices.

Obviously, no dog should be seen at a Howl-o-Ween sans costume. The National Retail Federation estimates that approximately one in ten pets dresses up for Halloween, so why not join the fun? Here are some popular ideas:

Pirate	Devil	Superhero
Pumpkin	Witch	Ghost
Clown	Princess	Angel

But if you're in a creative mood there's no need to feel restricted to store-bought outfits! You know your dog better than anyone. Does your golden look like a very large goldfish? Does your pug look like a bug? Maybe your dachshund looks like a hot dog in a bun or your Shih Tzu looks like Yoda.

Some puppy parents even choose to dress their pets in costumes that complement their own. The possibilities are endless, but here are some of my favorites:

Sonny & Cher
Santa & Rudolph
Pig & farmer
Little Red Riding Hood & the big, bad Wolf
Baby in a carriage & mother/father

Batman & Robin
Superman & Superwoman
Cowboy & Native American
Vampire & bat

Of course your guests will want to do more than just sit around looking spooky. Nothing says Howl-o-Ween like pumpkin carving. Have a competition to see who can get their jack-o'-lantern to look most like their pet. Or why not show off your houseful of costumed dogs by parading them around the neighborhood? Kids love to see dogs dressed up. If you're in the competitive mood, vote on your favorite (no hanging chads; recounts are technically acceptable, but by the time you're finished the dogs will all have managed to wriggle out of their costumes anyway). The winner can get a prize donated from a local pet vendor or have the honor of presenting the donated goods to your local shelter.

A gluttonous game for pups is Bark or Treat. Ask everyone to bring a package of their favorite dog treats. Dogs will be able to go from parent to parent, begging for a new treat—if you're like my parents when it comes to Halloween you'll save the treats to give out gradually over several days; if you're like me you'll let the dogs eat all of them then and there.

Planning Your Own Dog Wedding or Canine Commitment Ceremony

I know there are people who want to stick with traditional marriage, but I feel that if two dogs love each other, it's cruel to keep them apart simply because they have four legs and a tail. If your dog has found true love with another of his species, why not plan a ceremony for the adorable couple?

Just like a birthday paw-ty, a wedding can be themed. You can go traditional, cultural, or modern depending on the happy couple's tastes. The decorations will depend on your theme, whether it be a Red Rover Roses wedding, a beach wedding, or a traditional black and white wedding (great for Dalmatians).

Since all bitches have been dreaming of their wedding gown since puppyhood, put her in a white dress with a veil or train. White doggie brides can go the simple route and wear just a veil. For males, a tuxedo is the best idea. If your boy doesn't like putting on a full dinner jacket, you can purchase a cuffed collar and bow tie and cuffs for his legs. If he wants to be superchic, throw on a top hat to make him the star of his own wedding.

For the ceremony, it's probably going overboard to get a real minister, priest, or rabbi to marry the two love dogs, and anyway it would be far more meaningful if you led the ceremony yourself. Find a commitment ceremony text online and modify it for the occasion. This way your dog will know that when you give him away you're not really giving him away—you're just bringing new friends into his life.

To celebrate the union, have new dog

tags made up that feature the dogs' combined names. The new tags are something the dogs can wear everywhere and, as with a wedding ring, show their loyalty to each other.

Many gourmet bakeries will be more than happy to make a tiered doggie cake for your dog on his day. Or make a doggie meat loaf (page 17) or bake and decorate wedding-themed peanut butter treats (page 69). Be canine creative!

Marrying Your Breed and Your Brood

When I first adopted Lucky, I had no idea that the Maltese was a fearless, social, lively dog—I just knew in my heart that she was the right dog for me. After only a few weeks with Lucky, though, I realized that we had a lot in common: We're both friendly and energetic, we don't require a lot of exercise, and we both love shopping. I started to realize that Lucky would fit perfectly into my life.

Lady and the Tramp

I'm not the only big fan of the Maltese. Iconic actor Dame Elizabeth Taylor doesn't travel very far without her high-maintenance and pampered Maltese, Daisy. Taylor has quipped, "Some of my best leading men have been dogs and horses."

It's this effortless, instantaneous, unconditional bond—what I call puppy love—that leads people to choose their dogs no matter what the breed. If you haven't yet brought home a new best friend, it's a good idea to consider the personalities and needs of various breeds so you'll end up with a dog well suited to you and your family. If your four-legged sidekick is already firmly entrenched in your life, learning more about his breed will only enhance the time you spend together.

It's in the Breed

Whether your dog came from the pound or from a breeder, whether he's a mature gentleman or an inexhaustible puppy, whether you've had him for a few weeks or what feels like a few centuries, you've already stamped your mark on his personality. Not just the training you've given him but the atmosphere in your home, the way you and your family play with him, and the other people he

American Kennel Club Foundation Stock Service Dogs

Here is a partial list of some of the "rare breeds" trying to make it as an official breed under the restrictions of the American Kennel Club (I'm rooting for the Xoloitzcuintli, the oldest indigenous dog in the Americas!): American English coonhound, Argentine Dogo, Azawakh, Barbet, Belgian Laekenois, Boerboel, Bracco italiano, Cane Corso, Catahoula leopard dog, Cesky terrier, Chinook, Cirneco dell'Etna, Czechoslovakian Vlčák, Entlebucher mountain dog, Eurasier, Grand Basset Griffon Vendéen, Kai Ken, Kooikerhondje, Lagotto Romagnolo, Mudi, Norrbottensdogs, Peruvian Inca orchid, Pumi, Sloughi, Stabyhoun, Tosa, treeing Tennessee brindle, and Xoloitzcuintli.

meets—they all contribute to the formation of his character. There are, however, certain innate traits that dogs are born with regardless of how they're raised. This explains why even though Lucky enjoys running around decorously in the park, sniffing for gourmet bones, and taking a high-profile walk with me, she's sometimes wary of strangers. These characteristics depend on your dog's specific breed, and all dogs have them, from the Great Dane to the toy Chihuahua to mixed breeds—aka your everyday mutt.

The American Kennel Club (AKC) groups dog breeds into eight categories: sporting, hound, working, terrier, toy, herding, nonsporting, and miscellaneous. As of 2009, the AKC recognizes 161 dog breeds in its seven categories, as well as 11 breeds in a "miscellaneous" class. On top of those 172 breeds, they accept submissions from 64 breeds into their Foundation Stock Service, a program created for breeders who are trying to establish a breed in the United States. (They can do so only when there are 150 canines registered—these are some very rare breeds of dog!)

Historically, dogs have been bred for specific tasks, and they hold on to their ancestral instincts. So if you notice your cocker spaniel has a mysterious talent for hunting or your collie is a master at herding squirrels in your backyard, don't be alarmed; embrace his heritage. Lucky and I have put together a list of traits to help you understand your breed better and get some ideas about incorporating your pup's heritage into his everyday life.*

* Classification courtesy of AKC.org.

SPORTING (retriever, setter, spaniel, Weimaraner, pointer, Brittany)

Dogs that fall in the sporting group category were originally bred to hunt. They are wildly athletic and often love swimming and the outdoors. They make outstanding companions because of the parent–puppy bonding time during long hunts. Sporting dogs such as the golden retriever are often seen as the "all-American dog" (don't tell Lucky this). While they have a natural affinity to the outdoors, they are also adaptable to urban environments as long as they get plenty of exercise. A sporting dog would therefore be ideal for an active parent. Hunting (if you're so inclined), swimming, fetch, running, tap dancing, Pilates, rhythmic gymnastics, or anything else athletic is especially appropriate.

HOUND (greyhound, basset hound, Irish wolfhound, dachshund, beagle, whippit, saluki, harrier, Rhodesian ridgeback)

Any breed ending in "hound" is going to be a hound dog. Although the term "hound dog" has earned something of a derogatory meaning in recent history (thanks a lot, Elvis!), the hound dog has long been invaluable as a tracker. Many hounds have a keen sense of smell and a very distinct bark known as "baying." You may have heard your dog baying when a siren or other startling noise strikes his ear. Like sporting dogs, hounds adapt easily to different environments and enjoy exercise-heavy activities. If your dog is a sniffer, play a game in which you take five identical objects (like spoons), hold one for a long time, and put them in different places—he has to bring you back the one you handled. Play hide-and-seek with his favorite toy, or teach him other scents to track down.

WORKING (Siberian husky, Bernese mountain dog, black Russian terrier, Akita, mastiffs, Saint Bernard, Portuguese water dog, boxer, Doberman Pinscher, rottweiler, Samoyed, Newfoundland, Great Dane, schnauzer)

Dogs that fit in the working category have historically been trained to perform tasks to assist humans that can range anywhere from rescue to transportation. These are typically large, intelligent dogs that have incredible strength and endurance. If you're the parent of a working dog, then you know how essential it is that the dog be properly trained. Working dogs are for the strong-willed, patient parent and the laid-back kid. Like their mates in the larger dog categories, working dogs love strenuous activities that require a lot of endurance—you may find, in fact, that your dog's endurance far exceeds your own. Wilderness activities such as hiking, snowshoeing, and backpacking are a great start.

TERRIER (Airedale terrier, American Staffordshire terrier, Bedlington terrier, border terrier, bull terrier, Dandie Dinmont terrier, miniature schnauzer, Norfolk terrier, Norwich

terrier, Parson Russell terrier, Scottish terrier, Skye terrier, Welsh terrier, wire fox terrier)

Terriers come in all shapes, sizes, and colors. Terrier parents, no matter their dog's size or origin, are well aware of the terrier's distinct personality. He can be extremely stubborn and feisty, while running on constant high energy. Historically, terriers were used to track down and kill everyday pests, so they don't always get along with other animals, canine or otherwise. Because of the terrier's natural competitiveness, it's probably best to stick to activities that don't include other animals. Games with a terrier may be daunting because of his natural stubbornness, so it's important to train the terrier to understand the importance of reward for completing a task in order to maximize your terrier's active potential. The bottom line is: The busier you keep your terrier, the happier you two will be together.

TOY (Cavalier King Charles spaniel, Chihuahua, pug, Shih Tzu, Pekingese, Pomeranian, Maltese, poodle, Yorkshire terrier, miniature pinscher, Italian greyhound, papillon)

Toy dogs have been bred solely to provide what the AKC calls "sheer delight" in their parents. Their size makes them the easiest dogs to take care of (though of course there are small breeds in groups other than the toy category). It's important to remember, however, that although toy dogs are smaller, it doesn't mean their attitude will be, too. More than anything else, toy dogs enjoy hanging out with their parents. They do require exercise, but strenuous activity isn't their favorite. Many toy dog parents are able to incorporate their dogs into their everyday life with particular ease (take Lucky and me, for example). A toy dog will enjoy doing anything as long as you're involved, so an activity can be as simple as a car ride, shopping trip, or stroll around the neighborhood.

HERDING (Australian cattle dog, Australian shepherd, Canaan dog, Cardigan Welsh corgi, bearded collie, collie, German shepherd, Old English sheepdog, Pembroke Welsh corgi, Polish lowland sheepdog, Portuguese water dog, puli, Shetland sheepdog)

The herding dogs are the newest group to the AKC. These dogs used to be in the working group but now have their own classification because of their uncanny ability to organize, control, and, well, herd other animals. If you're in a multiple-animal home you might want to keep an eye out. I had a friend whose German shepherd herded kittens like he was Babe on a sheep farm. Herding dogs are easy to train and make great companions. See how your collie responds to a group of many docile animals. If he starts taking charge of them immediately, great! If he ignores them, chances are he'll still enjoy the same activities as dogs in the sporting and working groups. Herding dogs also distinguish particularly well between the sounds of different

commands. Try teaching yours commands like "come by" (herd the flock counterclockwise), "cast" (herd the flock into a group), "look back" (look for a missing animal), and "walk up" (move closer to the flock).

NONSPORTING (American Eskimo dog, bichon frise, Boston terrier, bulldog, Chinese shar-pei, Chow Chow, Dalmatian, French bulldog, Keeshond, Lhasa Apso, Lowchen, schipperke):

The nonsporting group is a wildly diverse one—sort of the dog-breed version of "etcetera." Because of this, it is hard to identify a group of characteristics common to all the dogs in the group. Because of the versatility of the nonsporting group, your best guide to what will make your Dalmatian or bulldog happy is going to be his behavior and his responses to things you try with him.

If the Dog Fits . . .

Breed trends, like other trends, from neon to faux fur, are constantly changing. Take a look at the most popular dog breeds in the United States as of 2009. (Note, though, that the following stats were created before the Obamas chose their "first dog" of the United States. The Portuguese water dog might

MOST POPULAR AMERICAN DOG BREEDS

	2009	1999
1	Labrador retriever	Labrador retriever
2	Golden retriever	Golden retriever
3	Yorkshire terrier	German shepherd
4	German shepherd	Dachshund
5	Beagle	Beagle
6	Dachshund	Poodle
7	Boxer	Chihuahua
8	Poodle	Rottweiler
9	Shih Tzu	Yorkshire terrier
10	Miniature schnauzer	Boxer

move up the ranks as one of America's favorite canines, thanks to Bo Obama.)

Designer Dogs

Designer dogs, also known as hybrid dogs, are a relatively new trend in breeding. Designer dogs have two purebred parents of different breeds. These hybrid pooches usually turn out to be a perfect blend of two purebred dogs, offering diverse personality traits due to the dual combination. Take a Bo-Dach for example—a Boston terrier and dachshund mix. Bo-Dachs combine the all-American, playful, and sometimes easily distracted nature of a Boston terrier with the curious, adventurous, family-man personality of a dachshund.

Celebrities, often big fans of being or having a one of a kind—or at least first of a kind—sometimes take the same attitude toward their dogs and look for these purebred combinations when searching for loyal companions who will give them unconditional love but won't bark to tabloids or gossip columnists about any of their parents' private matters, no matter how much Pupperoni they're offered. Sarah Palin is the perfect example—talk about somebody scrutinized by the tabloid and entertainment media! Sarah has a Pompapoo (half Pomeranian/half poodle) named Inde (as in "Independence"). If parents are anything like their pups, this would make Sarah charming and self-confident like a Pomeranian and smart and well-groomed like a poodle.

The cross-breeding trend was first recognized by the *Encyclopaedia Britannica* in the late twentieth century, when many breeders began mixing other dog breeds with poodles in hopes of creating a wider array of dogs with the poodle's hypoallergenic qualities. Along with numerous cross-breedings come numerous portmanteau names (words that blend two words together) that can be traced back all the way to Queen Elizabeth II's Dorgis (who are mixes of dachshunds and corgis). Now we have Labradoodles, mini-Goldendoodles, Snoodles, Cockapoos, and Pompapoos—and the names keep getting sillier. Lucky has been after me lately to get her a brother or sister who's a Shih Tzu crossed with a bulldog—I figure the result has to be a Bull Shih. I'm still thinking about that one.

Mixed Breeds

Especially if your dog is a rescue dog, you might not know exactly what breeds make up his family tree. Fear not: A dog is a dog no matter who his parents are. It's still a good idea, though, for you to track down the mix of breeds that make up your dog, so you can be aware of what to expect from him and make plans to handle any special needs he might have. For some dogs it's simple to trace back a lineage, but for others it can be harder to tell. Fortunately, your vet will probably be able to figure it out; if not, and you're really keen to know, you can have your dog's DNA tested to find out his heritage. Once you know where your darling pooch came from,

you can adapt your routine accordingly. In the rare case when a breed or breeds can't be identified, don't panic! All dogs need a healthy diet, daily exercise, and a loving environment, and you can definitely handle that.

Hypoallergenic Dogs

It's horrible that not all people are able to experience the love of a dog, but unfortunately some of us suffer from mild to severe allergies around furry ones. I will confess that over the years I have developed some animal allergies myself (which makes the life I've chosen interesting, to say the least), but Lucky, being a Maltese, is hypoallergenic, which means that my symptoms are greatly reduced around her. Less dander is just dandy. (As far as dating people with dog allergies, all I can say is that you need to let your conscience be your guide. I myself once broke up with a man because he was allergic to Cipriani pasta sauce, so you can imagine my ideas on the subject, but I understand that not everyone might feel the same way.)

If you're looking for a rescue dog but you have allergies, no problem: There are several organizations that cater to specific breeds. Visit animalfair.com for a list of these shelters that will let you have your dog and not sneeze at it, either. Before going out and rescuing your hypoallergenic dog, though, you need to understand that your life with one of these dogs won't be completely allergy-free: He'll simply produce less of the dog dander that affects allergy sufferers the most. The producers of the allergens in question are the sebaceous glands, and there's no such thing (yet) as a dog without sebaceous glands. Mitigating factors can include size (less surface area means fewer allergens), ability to shed (no shedding means no allergens left all over the place), pH level (different levels make the dander easier on the allergy victim), and even propensity to bark (dogs who bark less will produce less dander from their mouths).

And there's absolutely no need to feel embarrassed about wanting a hypoallergenic dog. The nation's first dog, Bo Obama, is a Portuguese water dog—one of the most hypoallergenic breeds around!

Hypoallergenic Dogs

Here is a partial list of some commonly known hypoallergenic dogs: Affenpinscher, Airedale terrier, basenji, bearded collie, bichon frise, Chinese crested, fox terrier, greyhound, goldendoodle, Maltese, poodle, Pomeranian, Portuguese water dog, Scottish terrier, Welsh terrier, and Yorkshire terrier.

A New Dog in the House?

If you decide it's time to add a new pup to the brood and you're looking for a special breed,

Lucky's Tips for a Hypoallergenic Dog Home

As a Maltese, I know what us hypoallergenic dogs bring to the table, and here are a few tips to keep us even more allergen- and dander-free!

- It is important to keep us clean. With frequent washing and grooming, you can keep allergies under control—as much as I hate to have to suggest it, you should definitely consult the vet with any questions or concerns on this one.
- Clean your home frequently to avoid excess dander. That means making sure to vacuum the house often and install a strong air filtration / circulation system.
- I don't like this idea at all, but Mom said I had to include it. If you must—for example, if you have a highly allergic guest—you can make certain areas in the house "no-dog zones." I hope that the disdain with which I write those words comes through on the page.
- If your allergies are still acting up despite all the above, consider allergy shots to prevent all those unwanted symptoms. Let's face it: We're worth it.

don't feel you have to go straight to the breeder to get the pick of the litter. It's a little known fact that almost any (nonrare) breed of dog can be rescued from special breed rescue organizations, or even, with a little Luck(y), through your local shelter. The process certainly isn't as easy as going straight to the breeder; however, saving a life definitely makes it worth the wait and effort.

Why go to a breeder to get a Gordon setter when you can get one through the Gordon Setter Club of America? Looking for a Maltese? The American Maltese Association can help you out. If you're more of a Polish lowland sheepdog kind of person, you ought to look into the American Polish Lowland Sheepdog Club. Check out animalfair.com to find adoption agencies and organizations that deal with particular breeds.

Never buy a dog from a store, no matter how cute the one wagging his tail in the window is. Some dog stores stock their cages with dogs from puppy mills—horrible dog-breeding "factories" where conditions are miserable and where dogs are inbred and face temperament issues and severe medical problems.

If you're overwhelmed by all the pure-bred rescue organizations and you're just looking for a loving dog to add to your home,

consider a trip to your local animal shelter. Shelters are always filled with loving animals who may not be pure when it comes to breed, but who never offer less than 100 percent pure love.

Internet Scams

Nonsecure Internet sites will often display advertisements looking to give purebred dogs for free to loving homes. The catch? They charge an "adoption fee"—for a dog that doesn't even exist. If you feel you have been a victim of a puppy scam, contact the Internet Crime Complaint Center and the Better Business Bureau.

If at First You Can't Rescue, Research, Research Again!

In the event that you can't find a rescue organization that has the New Guinea singing dog or Catahoula leopard dog you've been looking for, then it is time to contact a breeder. But you *must* do your research when looking for the right one. In addition to rescue information, the AKC has a database of breeders in its Breeder Referral Contacts to help you go about your search. Here are some suggestions, courtesy of the ASPCA (ASPCA.org), to make sure you're dealing with a reputable breeder.

- Always check references, including other customers who have purchased dogs from a specific breeder, as well as the veterinarian the breeder works with.
- Be sure to deal directly with a breeder, not a broker.
- Always visit. Reputable breeders and rescue groups will be more than happy to offer you a tour.
- If you are told that there will be no refunds for a sick puppy, you are most probably dealing with a puppy mill. A reputable breeder or rescue group will always take the puppy back, regardless of the reason.
- Always pick your puppy up at the kennel. Do not have the puppy shipped or meet at a random location.

Incorporating Your Pooch into the Family Brood

It doesn't take the Brady Bunch to tell you that combining families is hard. It may take weeks for your new dog to adjust to other dogs and humans in the household (and vice versa). Did you ever have an annoying roommate or noisy neighbor who drove you absolutely bonkers? Your new dog might feel just the same way—so a private area is an absolute necessity. A spare, low-traffic room where the dog can spend time away from people and other dogs is ideal, but even a doggie bed in a corner of a room will do.

Westminster—The Crème de la Crème of Canines

Just as humans have beauty competitions—from Miss America to local pageants featuring girls of all ages with spray tans hurling flaming batons—our dogs have a competition of their own—and it's been around far longer than any beauty pageant we know today. That "pageant" is known as the Westminster Dog Show. Established in 1877 by a group of sporting men inside a Manhattan bar, the Westminster is the second-longest-running continuously held sporting event in the country, right behind the Kentucky Derby—which started only one year earlier.

Each year over twenty-five-hundred dogtestants from over 160 breeds compete for multiple titles that include Best in Breed, Best in Group, and the most coveted of all: Best in Show. Christopher Guest fans will all know this popular phrase, which shares the name of one of my favorite movies. Parker Posey in her braces looking for Busy Bee gets me every time!

Also, the more consistent your dog's routine, the less stress he'll have to deal with. Anything you can do to cut down on doggie drama will be helpful.

Make sure to carve out special time for your dog, but also incorporate him in family activities and take him to the dog park to make his own friends.

Don't forget to doggie-proof your dog's new digs! To avoid a doggie disaster, make a clean sweep of your home and remove any dog hazards. Cover wires with tape, cap electrical outlets, keep cleaning products out of doggie reach. Take a look at the Section "Dog Safety Comes First," page 29, for more details.

A new dog requires some getting used to, and if you already have another dog, then you're not the only one who'll have to make this lifestyle adjustment. We all know that the bond you have with your dog is a strong one, so there will naturally be feelings of jealousy when another pup is thrown into the mix.

When introducing the two new furry friends destined to coexist, do so on neutral territory so that neither one feels threatened or has the upper paw. Make sure the tone you use with both of them is upbeat, and never forget to pay lots of attention to the dog who's been living with you for a while. Although you will be excited about your new dog, your trustworthy old friend will need more love and reassurance than ever so he

doesn't worry that an upstart is supplanting him in your affections. Rarely does anything go perfectly in life (although we mere mortals keep aspiring), so you must always be prepared for a little scuffle every now and then—a fight for top-dog status—but remain calm and they will work it out, learn to live together, and love each other as you love them both!

INTEGRATING YOUR NEW DOG INTO YOUR LIFESTYLE

SHOPPING TRIPS Name me one dog that doesn't enjoy a car ride! If you have a small dog, I say shed your fear and take her with you, as long as she is restricted inside a bag, coat, or carrier. If you know your town like I know mine, you'll know all the places your dog is allowed inside. Saks, Tiffany, Bloomingdale's, and Barneys, for example, all allow dogs inside their New York City locations, but IKEA doesn't, so make sure to call ahead. You don't want to show up for a day of window-shopping and people-and-dog-watching just to be turned away.

OUTSIDE EVENTS Outside events are the perfect place for a family gathering where everyone can participate—including the dogs. Family picnics, Fourth of July parties, or local outdoor concerts are all places you can tote your four-legged best friend along. It's very important to remember that not every event is for every breed—some dogs are afraid of fireworks and other loud noises. Before you go to a major Fourth of July display, test your dog by making a loud crackling sound and seeing how he reacts. If he runs under the bed and hides, it might be a better idea to watch the fireworks on TV.

NEIGHBORHOOD STROLLS If you need to go to the store right around the corner, why drive? Take your dog the long way and enjoy the walk together. If you need just one thing and the store doesn't allow dogs, tie him up outside for a minute. When you come out of the store, chances are there will be a gaggle of envious admirers gathered around him. Pretend not to feel superior that you have such a gorgeous dog and they don't. Just be very careful that while you're inside you keep an eye on your furry sidekick every once in a while. It seems unthinkable that somebody could be so cruel as to steal another person's dog, but it does happen. Don't let it happen to you.

DOG STORES Dog stores are one of the few places where it's a faux paw not to allow your four-legged friend inside with open arms. Next time you hit up your local dog store, bring your dog along with you. Just make sure your dog doesn't snag too many treat samples when no one is looking.

DINING Dining with your dog can be as easy as picking up the phone. During warmer weather, many restaurants offer outdoor seating where dogs are as welcome as patrons. Just make sure you phone ahead and

What's in a Dog's Name?

Choose a moniker that suits not only your dog's stellar personality and naturally good looks but also his surroundings and environment. Don't forget to make it fun and simple for your pup to remember. For example, I guarantee that if you name your dog Saturday Night Live because you rescued your new dog on a Saturday night and he's lively, you'll end up calling him "Night."

America's number-one dog name for many years in a row has been Lucky. Years ago, when I named my Lucky, picking a popular name was not on my mind—I just felt so lucky to have rescued the little dog who I knew would change my life. As much as she'd like to, Lucky Diamond can't take credit for the popularity of her name (although her appearances on the *Today Show* and *Greatest American Dog* show may certainly have inspired a viewer or two). I just think that all the parents who name their dogs Lucky must feel as fortunate as I do.

say you have a dog (and what type), and ask whether they offer any dog-friendly amenities like a water bowl or treats or whether you should bring your own.

Dogs and Kids

Bringing a dog and a child together in the home isn't always what you planned on. The day when I have to tell Lucky to sit still so she can hear the breaking news that a baby is coming into our home and our lives, she'll be in shock and head straight for the wee-wee pad. But there are certain steps you can take to make the transition easier for everyone involved, dogs and children alike.

Dogs, especially small dogs, can find children threatening, because they operate at eye level, have high-pitched voices, move quickly, and can be very unpredictable. Make sure to teach your children that they need to be gentle with animals and that dogs don't like to be bothered when eating or sleeping. (You can do your best to teach them that *you* don't like to be bothered when eating or sleeping, either, but to be honest I don't know how much luck you'll have with that.) Always supervise the interaction between your child and dog—you never really know what nefarious plots either one of them has in mind.

If you are expecting a child, do everything you can during your pregnancy to prepare your four-pawed buddy for the two-footed bundle of joy you'll be bringing home. If possible, bring a friend's child around so your dog will know what to expect and get used to sharing your coveted attention. Gently touch or poke all over your dog's

Dear Lucky

Dear Lucky,

I am a young, adorable German shepherd with a problem. My mother and father love me dearly, and do almost everything with me, but when we're all in bed together, it seems like three's a crowd. Oftentimes Dad is out of town and Mom lets me sleep with her, but when he gets back he barks about how crowded the bed is and it's back to the floor for me. I don't understand. Help!

Heidi
Oklahoma City, Oklahoma

Dear Heidi,

You are definitely in a pickle! I can offer you two different ways to go about solving your problem. Obviously, your mother already knows the importance of incorporating you into her everyday family life, but it is taking your father a little longer. If you're on the bed, show Mom and Dad that you don't have to take up so much room and that you won't be too much of a disturbance to their normal sleep. Hide at the end of the bed, or nestle up to Mom where you know you're welcome. If this still doesn't work, ask your folks to get you a really comfy dog bed.

Good luck!

Yours truly,

Lucky

body to see if there is a certain area that you will have to warn your child to stay away from. Teach your dog to give up his toy or food willingly if a human hand comes after it, because we all know how curious children are always reaching for things.

During your pregnancy, start to modify your pooch's routine little by little; that way, the change in his lifestyle won't be so abrupt, and he won't chase his tail in confusion and frustration for weeks on end. Many vets recommend gradually spending a little less time

with your dog. Let's face it: Babies are a lot of work, and you won't have quite as much time to spend with your hairier child. Buy or download a recording of a child crying or laughing, and play it softly for your dog. This will get your dog used to the sound of a baby's cry (some dogs get frightened by the sound) before the actual baby arrives. When the baby is born, consider bringing some baby clothes back from the hospital so your dog can get used to the scent before the bundle of joy arrives.

Most important, brush up on basic commands like "no," "stay," and "get down" so that you never have to worry about your pup tackling your child like a linebacker when issues of territory come up. You might even want to teach your pup to walk a little ahead of you, especially when going up or down the staircase, so you don't have to worry about him being underfoot and causing little people to fall.

It's a hard truth to face, but not all dogs are fit for all young children. Certain breeds, like the dingo, the Sarplaninac, or the New Guinea singing dog, simply aren't good around children. Numerous things can spark an unwanted dog attack, and if the breed isn't properly socialized, then your child may be in danger. Herding dogs may be mouthy, terriers can be very territorial, and some dogs may even mistake a child's cry for the sound of wounded prey. This doesn't mean that if you have a terrier or a corgi you necessarily have to shelve your plans for having kids—just make sure to consult your veterinarian and perhaps a trusted trainer to see how the two species may live together.

Also consider the temperament of specific dogs. Golden retrievers and Labs have well-deserved reputations as family dogs, but every once in a while you meet one whose instincts are aggressive. (You can usually tell because he'll be wearing a trench coat and dark glasses.)

It is important that both your child and your dog learn to respect each other. Any child incapable of handling a dog alone—toddlers tend to fit this description—should be supervised while with the family dog. When you're not there to keep an eye out, separate the child and the dog using gates or pens.

Good-byes and Farewells

There comes a time in everyone's life—woman, man, or dog—when the curtain will fall. The truth is that the loss of a dog can be as traumatic as the loss of a human family member. Depending on your relationship with the dog, you may experience the same feelings of grief and depression. These feelings are completely natural and you should acknowledge them, not be ashamed of them or bottle them up. It's important to reach out to loved ones who understand the difficult time you're having. Many humane societies may even refer you to a dog-loss hotline or dog-loss support groups where you can share your feelings and fond memories with people in the same situation. It might also be useful

Top Ten Kid-Friendly Dogs

Golden/Labrador Retrievers Retrievers are the most popular family dogs in America. Not only are they good-natured, active, and loving creatures, but they are patient and loyal to their owners and their children. They can also be very affectionate.

Beagles Like the retrievers, beagles are very tolerant with children. Though they are bred for hunting and fishing, they can handle romping, active children. They are also very friendly with other animals and adapt well to their environment.

Collie The famous Lassie was a prime example of a great collie. Collies are good family pets, gentle, smart, and easy to train. Collies are also protective and will cuddle up to your children.

Great Dane Though their outward appearance can seem forbidding, Great Danes are very patient and extremely gentle around children. They are often referred to as "gentle giants." They can also be protective, and they make great guard dogs.

Pugs Pugs are very social creatures. Though their faces are scrunched and serious, they are playful and clever, and are known to be very obedient. They are also very attentive to their owners and can keep up with any active child.

Vizsla Though not as well known as the other dogs on this list, Vizslas are very gentle, loyal, and affectionate pets, attentive to children of all sizes. The Vizsla is also quiet, obedient, and smart, and can adapt to its surroundings quickly.

Bulldog Not to be confused with the pit bull, the bulldog is a very devoted, obedient, and patient animal. Though it is always willing to please, the bulldog preserves its own independence. The bulldog is patient and affectionate with children and strangers. It can be a very charming and comical animal.

Cocker Spaniel A cocker spaniel is possibly the most playful and outgoing breed known to man. Cocker spaniels are very smart and loyal to their owners, and can even be a bit overprotective when meeting strangers. They are sensitive creatures, but will not challenge the authority of their parents. They also live well with other pets.

Goldendoodle This golden retriever–poodle mix is a great dog for families with allergies. The hybrid pup is very sharp and loyal, and learns quickly. Obedience comes naturally, and goldendoodles love to interact, so they respond well to commands. They will be friendly and playful with your children, other pets, and guests.

Boxer Boxers are known for being playful and active. They are ready to pounce and play with you at the drop of a hat, and are very affectionate. Boxers are great guardians and will be your most loyal best friend. They are gentle with children and tend to be ideal playmates for larger kids.

to keep a diary about your thoughts and even, if you're so inclined, to create a memorial for your dog so you'll always have something tangible to bring back the amazing times you had with your best friend. In 1990 Pope John Paul II declared that "animals possess a soul and . . . men must love and feel solidarity with our smaller brethren." When animals leave this world, they too are welcomed at the Pearly Gates—almost certainly with treats the likes of which they never tasted on earth.

Mutt Makeover

Just like so many other aspects of dog parenthood, giving your dog a bath is no longer the stressful chore it used to be. Whether you've just taken him home from the animal shelter and he needs a little sprucing up or your precious pup is dirty after a romp in the park, cleaning and grooming can be not only easy but fun.

Before we get to the good stuff, though, Lucky and I have a few words of warning. First, human grooming products should never be used on animals. Our skin has a different pH level than that of our beloved four-leggeds, so be sure you are using products made just for dogs—and even then an allergic reaction is possible. Just as with humans, different kinds of dogs have different skin and fur. There is no product that will be right for every dog. If your dog develops a reaction (like red, itchy, or excessively dry skin), call your veterinarian immediately. In most cases, switching products will solve the problem. If you know your pup has oh-so-sensitive skin, you're in luck, because there are some great products made just for sensitive pooches. (I'm talking about sensitive *skin* here. If your dog is prone to hurt feelings, what you need is not shampoo, but either more quality time together or a dog therapist! Without her therapist, my little Lucky would never have worked through abandonment issues from her first parent.)

Now that we've gotten that out of the way, grab that doggie shampoo, your doggie clippers, and an old doggie towel from the garage—don't forget to bring your doggie while you're at it—and let's get grooming!

What Kind of Grooming Does My Dog Need?

So you've decided that your best buddy needs a makeover, but you don't know where to start. Well, not all doggie dos are created equal. If you are the proud parent of a poodle, your grooming regimen is going to be very different than if you have a short-haired, low-maintenance-coat pup. You'll need to adjust your grooming style depending on the texture, length, and sometimes even color of your dog's fur. Some dog breeds might require a simple bath, while others (like my high-maintenance Lucky) need a bath, flea bath, blow-dry, clipping, coat gloss, and a stylish new scarf around the neck to top it off. (I've tried it without the stylish new scarf. I think it's better that I not go into specifics, but let's just say that reupholstering your entire living room is even less fun than you think it'd be.) In general, dogs with short, smooth coats are fairly low maintenance as far as grooming goes, although some short-coated breeds, like the Chinese shar-pei and the Dogue de Bordeaux, have extremely sensitive skin that needs special attention. If there are grooming essentials you need to know, your vet will tell you.

When Does My Dog Need Grooming?

Although there is no hard-and-fast rule for how often to bathe your dog, the two most important considerations are (1) what type of coat your dog has and (2) how dirty he gets. Dogs with short hair might need a bath only every couple of weeks (three or four weeks is usually maximum), while dogs with curly, wiry, long, or otherwise high-maintenance coats might need weekly time with Mr. Rubber Duckie. A crucial point to consider when determining how often to bathe your pooch is your dog's activities and how dirty he gets while doing them. If your Princess Penelope the Pug rarely gets a paw dirty, she will not need to bathe as frequently as her neighbor Buzz the Boston Terrier who likes to roll

Hardest-to-Easiest Dogs to Groom

If you're a proud parent of one of these breeds, you may need to seek out professional assistance (hardest): Afghan hound, Finnish spitz, Lhasa Apso, cocker spaniel, Pekingese, Chow Chow, Maltese, bichon frise, Chinese shar-pei, Alaskan malamute, Dogue de Bordeaux, Newfoundland.

Read up on these breeds and you'll be grooming at home in no time (moderate): Akita, collie, Jack Russell terrier, Saint Bernard, Old English sheepdog, border terrier, Irish setter, Maltipoo, mastiff, golden retriever, pug, beagle, Labrador retriever, papillon, basenji, bulldog, Welsh terrier.

It's a grooming walk in the park for these breeds (easiest): Boston terrier, boxer, pit bull, pointer, Doberman pinscher, Dalmatian, Weimaraner, whippet, Great Dane, Rottweiler, Chihuahua, French bulldog, Rhodesian ridgeback.

around in dirt and the occasional pigeon droppings in the park. (And you wonder why Penelope and Buzz never got together.) All dogs require more bathing attention during the summer to avoid tick or flea problems; during winter, it's especially important to dry your dog properly to prevent moist eczema.

Often the best way to determine whether your dog's do is due for a shampoo is the good old-fashioned smell test—the same one we used on our laundry in college. In general, however, the fewer baths you give, the better, within reason. Bathing dogs strips their coats of natural healthy oils, and some dogs have sensitive and/or allergic skin that does not react well to frequent bathing. If your companion is a puppy (younger than eight weeks old), you should avoid bathing him at all—puppies have extraordinarily sensitive skin—unless he's particularly dirty, in which case you should wash him in the sink with lukewarm water (not hot), or even safer, give him a sponge bath or wipe down with a yummy-smelling puppy wipe. At the same time, don't wait too long to bathe your dog. Once the eight-week mark has hit, it's important for a puppy to have his first bath as soon as possible so he can get accustomed to soapy water fun before he grows hardened in his ways (the old dog new tricks theory). If you use a gentle puppy shampoo, your little pup won't even know the difference between soap and water.

Grooming Guffaws

Let's face it: We can't all be great at everything we try. I, for example, cannot make brownies to save my life. They're horrible. Not food-poisoning horrible, but close. What I'm getting at is that grooming at home may not be for everyone. There is no shame in putting the shampoo and scissors down and taking your beloved pooch to your local groomer or veterinarian. I don't want any of your dogs to end up like my friend Rex's poor terrier, Sasha. Rex was determined to give her an at-home haircut and she couldn't show her snout at the dog park for months, out of "shear" embarrassment. If you aren't comfortable grooming at home, it's best to leave it to the professionals, especially if your dog requires cutting or clipping. A nervous human, a hyperactive dog, and a sharp pair of scissors make for a less than attractive combination. Remember to make safe, sensible choices! Even if you've always dreamed of creating an at-home spa experience for your dog, if it's not practical, you might need to shelve that dream and take up knitting.

Another important issue to consider before you begin grooming is space. If you have a Saint Bernard and a small upright shower, bathing your buddy at home might not be the best idea. Fortunately, many doggie spas, dog stores, and doggie day-care facilities now offer do-it-yourself bathing centers featuring raised tubs that allow you to stand comfortably while bathing your furry

friend—and stairs that can help you get your pooch into the bath in the first place. If you have a giant breed dog, you might save yourself a serious backache by heading to one of these facilities. These self-service centers, located in nearly every state from Mud Puppies in Austin, Texas, to Dippity Do Dog in Chandler, Arizona, to Birch Bay Dirty Dog Wash in Blaine, Washington, can offer the best of both worlds—you get to bathe and bond with your dog in a space that was made for dog grooming, and your home won't start to look like the set of *Mission: Impossible* after all the bombs have gone off. Furthermore, there will be an extra pair of hands on deck in case your pooch decides to make a break for it mid-shampoo.

The final grooming factor you need to consider is the most important one: your dog himself. Some dogs might be uncomfortable with water, scissors, or both. I have seen some poor dogs actually become aggressive at the sight of water (*such* a cat thing to do). If your dog seems excessively scared, nervous, or upset when he sees you preparing the tub or taking out the scissors for some grooming *à deux*, it is best to halt the production. You can discuss alternatives with your vet or groomer. In some extreme circumstances, a dog might need a sedative in order to get the grooming he needs. The worst thing that you can do is force your dog into a situation that could end up harming him or you. The point of grooming is to pamper your dog and provide you and your dog a way to bond. If there are dog fears and human tears involved, something has gone awry!

Rub-A-Dub-Dub: A Human, a Dog, and a Tub

If you decide that an at-home bath is the path for you, you have several options. If you are working with a small breed dog, the sink might be the best venue for the imminent scrubbing. If your dog won't fit in the sink, however—and sometimes even if he will—you're going to want to take him either to the tub or outside. Here are some pluses and minuses of all three:

SINK One of the first of many benefits of a sink wash is that you can stand up and easily give your dog some soapy TLC. You can also lay out towels, combs, and any other essential supplies on the counter where they can be easily reached. If you are washing your dog in the kitchen sink, however, there is one obvious downside—you are washing your dog in the kitchen sink. Obviously, you need to clean the area thoroughly when you're done. I love my Lucky to pieces, but I don't want her luscious white locks to end up in my next meal.

BATHTUB If you use the tub, you have more space—not only more space for your dog, but also more space for you to maneuver. My friend Sally sits on the edge of the tub with her feet in the water while she washes her beagle, Mr. Chips. Sitting on the edge of the tub during the bath can help your dog feel more secure, prevent him from dashing midway through his bath (you serve as a barrier), and spare you some serious back

pain and your floor an unnatural flood. One downside of the tub is that it is potentially messier. Since there is more space for your dog to wriggle around in, you should expect things to get a little wet—that includes you, the walls, and the floor. Make sure to have ample towels everywhere.

OUTSIDE If indoor bathing isn't your thing (and trust me, cleaning up a kitchen or bathroom post-bath is even less fun than you think it is), outdoor bathing—preferably next to a white picket fence—might be just what the beautician ordered. The trick here is to keep your dog from running away and/or bathing you (whichever might come first). Ideally, you can be in an enclosed area (like a backyard) so that if your dog does slip away from you, there won't be any unfortunate accidents. Even if you have a fenced-in yard, however, you should always use a collar and leash; try holding the leash with one hand while wetting, shampooing and rinsing with the other. To protect your yard and your neighborhood's ecology, it is ideal to wash your dog where the runoff can go down a grate or drain. And make sure to bathe your dog only in mild to warm temperatures—neither you nor your dog will enjoy being wet, cold, and outside during cooler months. If it's too cold for you to go swimming outside, it's probably too cold for his bath.

No matter where you wash your dog, Lucky and I have a few tips to make the process a smooth one. First, have all of your supplies ready before you begin. That means you should have your dog shampoo, conditioner, detangler, and any other products you plan to use on hand. You should also have towels—and lots of them—ready to go. Wear old clothes that you don't mind getting wet; you might even consider investing in a plastic apron to wear while bathing your baby. Or, if you're like my friend Miranda, you can

Dry Your Dog with Ease!

Congratulations—you finished the actual bath! Now you just need to dry your dog. Allow him to shake off—it might be messy, but it is a dog's natural instinct and gets rid of excess water in a flash. Try holding up a towel to shield your walls and floor from getting wet. After the shake-off, begin patting your dog gently with towels. Then rub your dog's skin gently in a circular motion. Some dogs can air-dry in minutes, but others might require the help of a dryer. Many professional groomers use large fan-style dryers, but a home hair dryer set on the lowest heat can also work. Hold the dryer approximately twelve inches away from your dog and take frequent breaks to make sure neither his skin nor his patience is getting irritated.

do all your dog washing in a bikini in the front yard. Have some treats on hand to keep your pooch preoccupied during the process—with the help of a tasty snack, your dog might actually come to look forward to bath time.

Choices, Choices, Choices: What to Wash Your Canine With

If you think the shampoo aisle of your local drugstore is enough to make your head spin, stay away from the doggie shampoo aisle of your local dog emporium. As deliciously delectable as they may seem, try to avoid dog products that have fragrances, dyes, and unnatural additives. Harsh chemicals and your pup's skin are a terrible combination. I have a general rule of thumb—if I can't pronounce it, it doesn't go near Lucky. Look for products that feature natural, organic elements like avocado oil, oatmeal, tea tree, fucus, horsetail, and spirulina, all of which help many dogs maintain healthy skin and coats. In addition to looking for natural, organic ingredients, you should also try to select products that feature vitamins, especially vitamin E, which can help soothe your dog's skin. If you find a shampoo that includes therapeutic essential oils it may even calm *you* down in stressful bathing situations.

Is Shampoo Enough? Conditioners, Detanglers, and Sprays

For many dogs, a quality shampoo is all the product that they will need. However, if your dog has long, coarse, or wiry hair, you might also want to use some conditioner. Conditioners can add extra moisture to dry, itchy skin; they can also be used to help work through mats or thick tangles. Detanglers are like conditioners but are not rinsed out with water. If your best friend's coat has somehow gotten extremely matted, you might need to use a combination of conditioner and detangler in order for his hair to be tangle-free.

Fucus, Horsetail, and Spirulina

While all dogs can benefit from products that are chock-full of natural ingredients and vitamins, some dogs might require specialty products. If your baby has dry, itching, red, or flaky skin, he could likely benefit from an extra-delicate shampoo made just for dogs with sensitive skin and allergies. Aloe vera and tea tree oil shampoos, for example, will probably dispense with his case of the itchies right away. If his coat is continually itchy, dry, or sensitive, it is a good idea to talk with your vet. She might suggest a vitamin supplement or another solution to help soothe your dog's skin.

Dear Lucky

Dear Lucky,

Whenever I see pictures of you in the tabloids, I notice that your coat is always so white and bright! Mine is always dull and dingy. How can I get your look?

Lackluster
Las Vegas, Nevada

Dear Lackluster,

Here's the shampoo scoop! I use a special shampoo just for us canines that have light fur. Look for shampoos made specifically for white pups in the grooming aisle at the pet store. You also have to worry about those pestilent tearstains. It helps to drink spring water rather than tap, but if staining remains a problem, have your mom or pop take you to the vet and they can prescribe you something like tetracycline, Gentian Violet Flush, or lincocin. Good luck staying bright—and next time you write, I hope you sign your note "Luster"!

Yours truly,

Lucky

Just as with shampoos, pick conditioners and detanglers made with natural, organic ingredients that will leave your dog's coat feeling healthy and looking shiny.

The Nitty Gritty: Ears, Nails, and Teeth

Thought you were done when the shampoo was rinsed out and the dog was dried off? Think again! There are three more vital aspects to your dog's grooming routine. The first is ear cleaning. Fold back your pup's ears and you might notice a dark waxy substance. That is dog earwax, and it's gotta go! Cleaning your dog's ears may not be as much fun as a sudsy bath—for you or your dog—but it's simple and quick. Fold back the ear and gently swab the outer areas with a thin cloth or paper towel (never a Q-tip). Never, ever enter the ear canal! If a paper towel isn't doing it for you, you can get premoistened cloths at the dog store, made with organic aloe, witch hazel, apple cider, and other natural ingredients. Regular ear cleanings prevent

odor, infection, and that unsightly wax buildup!

Nail trims can be tricky, so if you don't feel comfortable, ask your veterinarian or a professional groomer to handle this step. Overgrown nails can break in ways that are painful to dogs, and long-term overgrowth can lead to soreness, difficulty walking, and even arthritis, so you should make sure your dog's nails are trimmed by *somebody*. There are two parts of the nail—a thick outer layer and a softer, highly sensitive inner layer called the quick. If your dog has light-colored nails, you can actually see the quick. It is pinkish in color and is shorter than the outer layer.

The secret to clipping a dog's nails is to avoid the quick at all costs. You've undoubtedly heard the expression "cut to the quick"—there's a reason it connotes pain. So go slow. With dog nail clippers (don't attempt to cut a dog's nails with human clippers) clip very small amounts off of the tip of the nail. Dogs' nails are much thicker than humans', so this could be a challenge. Just remember that less is best! You might need to cut the nails over several days to achieve the desired length, but cutting a little at a time is the safest way to avoid hurting your baby.

If you do clip the quick, it is extremely painful for your dog and he will probably bleed. You should always have styptic powder on hand; it's available at any dog store. Simply apply the powder to the nail and start with lots of apologies and promises of extra treats!

The final dog grooming procedure we'll discuss is admittedly Lucky's *least* favorite: teeth brushing. Your dog might not love to get his teeth brushed, but regular brushings are essential and can prevent serious tooth decay and other problems that are painful for your dog and your wallet. If you begin a tooth-brushing routine at an early age, your dog will become accustomed to the process. The good news is that there are lots of toothpastes in dog-irresistible flavors like beef and chicken. Before introducing the toothbrush into your pup's mouth, put some of the toothpaste on your finger and let him get a good taste of what's to come. Slowly introduce the toothbrush and keep the toothpaste coming. If you see that your dog has serious tooth decay or seems to be in pain when you

What About Dental Treats?

There are lots of doggie dental treats on the market. These are treats that claim to help your dog reduce tooth plaque and maintain fresh breath. Dental treats can be effective but should not be used as a replacement for brushing. If your dog won't let you anywhere near her with a toothbrush in hand, dental treats may be your best option in between visits to the vet—just remember: not too many!

brush, you should have him checked out at the veterinarian. Dental problems in canines are serious. Even if you brush at home, some dogs build up excess plaque that your vet will need to remove with special (and expensive) procedures and tools. Certain breeds—such as pugs, Pomeranians, Maltese (trust me—I know, because of my little Lucky), and Yorkies in particular—are particularly prone to tooth decay, so dental health is vital for these pups. They need their teeth to chew the delicious treats you give them!

Canine Coiffures

There are certainly pluses and minuses of both at-home and professional canine coiffures. At-home jobs can be less expensive but also riskier. Your dog could end up with a botched cut and, in extreme cases, an injury. If you plan to give your dog an at-home cut, you should be able to answer a resounding yes! to the following questions:

1. Do I feel comfortable handling scissors or clippers around my dog?
2. Is my dog calm enough that I can safely use scissors or clippers around her?

If your answer is less than enthusiastic to these two crucial questions, I suggest that you leave cutting, clipping, shearing, and shaving to professionals (and don't worry—we have some tips to help you find the best groomer for you and your dog). However, if you feel like an at-home cut is the route for you and your pup, here's how you should proceed.

AT-HOME HAIRCUTS

The first step is to set up a clean work area and have all of your supplies (scissors, towels, treats, other grooming products, etc.) within reach. Allow yourself plenty of time. If you think the cut will take thirty minutes, schedule an hour. You don't want to be rushed when your dog and scissors are involved.

CUTTING HAIR You will need to invest in a high-quality pair of grooming scissors. If you use nonspecialty scissors, you and your dog will both regret it. You need a sharp, special pair just for your furry friend. Before you make the first cut, you need to decide how much length you are going to take off. If this is your first time cutting your dog's hair, you should plan on no more than a trim. Then, as you and your dog become more comfortable, you can begin to remove more length. It is always preferable to cut less than you think is necessary the first time around. As my hairstylist says, going back and taking more hair off is a heck of a lot easier than going back and taking less hair off. Go slowly; take your time and call on your inner perfectionist when you're cutting your dog's hair.

SHAVING HAIR For some canines, a trim or cut will not do—in the summer months, a full shave is essential for thick-coated pooches. You will need to invest in quality shears that come with a variety of guards. The higher quality shaver you buy, the more pleasant the experience will be. Pick a guard length that corresponds to your dog's coat length. Try an

Lucky's Tips: Finding the Groomer That Suits You

(and your parent) . . .

We girls know it can be difficult to find the right person for the right job, especially when it comes to personal services. I once had three different dog walkers in one week because none of them would adjust to my pace. Hello . . . I'm a Maltese with little legs. Do I look like a greyhound? But finding the right groomer doesn't have to be a pain in your paw if you follow a few of my tips.

1. Find a licensed and insured dog groomer. Dog grooming can be a bit expensive, but the only thing that should be cut here is your hair—not corners. You need a groomer who has been trained and licensed to work with animals like you. Ask your canine friends whose coats you've always admired where they got their work done (or have your human ask theirs). You can also have your human ask your vet for some suggestions. Your groomer should also be insured—unfortunately, humans can have accidents almost as easily as dogs, and you need to make sure you are covered.

2. Depending on your breed, coat length, and texture, you need to decide on a suitable style. If you're an English bulldog, don't expect to emerge from the groomer with a poodle's curls. Always consider the season, as well: If you're an Old English sheepdog you might love your long, thick locks, but in the summertime a shave is necessary to prevent overheating and dehydration.

3. Communication! Whether you want your groomer simply to bathe you or give you an all-over cut and style (spa day!), you and your human need to communicate with the groomer. Even a professional can't read minds, unless she is a professional dog clairvoyant, but those are extremely hard to come by. Let your groomer know exactly what you want so she can meet your needs. If you are expecting to emerge from the doggie salon with matching yellow bows in your ears, let the groomer know! A good groomer will be happy for you and your parent's input and direction, and a great groomer will have plenty of colorful bows.

inch guard to remove long hair and then move on to a smaller guard to get the close cut you desire. Before you begin shaving your dog, you should acclimate him to the sound of the clippers. Begin shaving on the back and move toward your dog's face and feet. Just like when you are using scissors, an even shave is your goal. It is always better to leave your dog's hair a little longer than to end up with an uneven, botched shave, unless you're going for a punk-rocker look, in which case your best bet is probably to use a blindfold.

PROFESSIONAL HAIRCUTS

There are a few main venues for professional doggie haircuts. The first is at the veterinarian (many vets have a groomer on hand at least a couple of days a week). Or you can take your pal to a dog store that offers grooming or grooming facilities. Some cities even have mobile dog groomers that will come with their fully equipped grooming vehicles to your home. I haven't convinced one to bring ice cream along, but I have not yet begun to fight.

Happy Grooming to You . . .

Giving your baby a makeover is not just a soap-and-water affair—it can truly be a bonding extravaganza. Just make choices that are best for you and your dog so you avoid scissor snafus and petrified pups. Approach bathing and grooming your dog as a way to show your love and devotion—who could ask for anything more?

Fashion Has Gone to the Dogs!

In 1999, when I created *Animal Fair,* the premier pet-lifestyle magazine and website, I wanted to kick the launch off with a loud bark, so I got in touch with a bunch of celebrities who generously agreed to perform dog-walking duties for the event. But then I started worrying that the dogs would feel miffed at being outshone by the glamorously dressed celebrities, so I thought, why don't we get famous fashion designers to design one-of-a-kind dog outfits to match our celebrity dog walkers?

The next thing you know, I was producing Paws for Style, the first dog fashion show designed to raise money and awareness for animal rescue—to this day it's still one of the most talked-about annual animal charity events: *where dogs take over the catwalk.* The fashion world has proven to be the source of an incredible amount of support for the animal rescue community, and an impressive list of designers have adorned the dogs in creative attire for this one-of-a-kind canine charity event, including Marc Jacobs, Gucci, Dolce & Gabbana, Burberry, Chaiken, Coach, Randolph Duke, Tommy Hilfiger, Betsy Johnson, Donna Karan, Todd Oldham, Alice Roi, Kate Spade, Vivienne Tam, Richard Tyler, and Vera Wang, to name a few. Celebrity dog walkers have included Hayden Panettiere, Cornelia Guest, Hilary and Haylie Duff, Vanessa Trump, Carson Kressley, Thom Filicia and Jai Rodriguez from *Queer Eye,* Paula Abdul, Hugh Hefner and the girls, Gabriel Byrne, Rob Thomas from Matchbox Twenty, Vanessa Williams, Hilary Swank, Veronica Webb, and a bevy of Ford Model beauties!

When I started Paws for Style, canine couture and dog product lines were a rare breed. At this time, not even Juicy Couture had a dog line; there were fewer than a half-dozen designers making dog outfits. Pet stores offered maybe one or two dog clothing items, not the entire designer doggie sections you see today. The *New York Times* had us on the front page of its Style section; this created a dog fashion buzz heard round the world by canines who yearned to be more fashionable and by the designers who loved them. What a difference a decade makes, especially when it starts with charity! Humane societies across the country are hosting their own Paws for Style events, and now there's even a Dog Fashion Week in the United States—and one in China!

I've seen everything from border collies in frilly pink dresses and boas to dachshunds in Halloween hot dog outfits, and it just keeps getting more extreme. Sometimes Lucky and I agree that the effect of a doggie outfit is stunning, but every once in a while she'll turn to me and raise and eyebrow, and I know what she's thinking: Enough is enough.

So she thought it would be a good idea to offer a few dog fashion guidelines. While no harm is done by dressing your dog for inclement weather or decking him in the occasional outfit for only a few hours at special occasions such as a wedding, dog Halloween costume party, Toys for Dogs holiday event, Yappy Hour benefit party, or any charity event that raises money for homeless animals or underdog causes, dressing up your animal on an everyday basis is like wearing a couture dress to lounge around the house—there are simply better and more natural things to spend your time on.

When it's not okay to dress up your dog:

- Breakfast/lunch/dinner
- Dog park
- Hiking (unless it's Mt. Everest)
- Doctor's appointment
- Every day

Doggie Fashion Trends

Whether it's LA, New York, or New Orleans, when Lucky and I are working the doggie red carpet, I'm amazed that there are no catfights over who's the best dressed! Prada, Gucci, Burberry—it's like an animal spread in *Vogue* magazine wherever I go!

There are now hundreds of companies offering apparel and accessories! Ralph Lauren, Juicy Couture, Hermès, Burberry, Coach, Kate Spade, Gucci, and Prada are just some of the high-end companies that offer or have offered dog clothing or accessory lines.

History

Lucky and I aced our exams in doggie fashion history, so you can trust us to give you the real story. If you can believe it, people started dressing their canines as far back as AD 520 to protect them from the wars. (Lucky says she bets those warriors looked so cute and strong in their tiny chain mail. She suggested bringing it back as a fashion trend, but I disapprove, as it doesn't come in different colors for day and evening.)

Silver dog collars have been dated back to the 1600s, but these were mostly available only to aristocrats and royalty. In the early 1790s, wealthy owners began to dress dogs in gold collars bejeweled with semiprecious stones. (Lucky is a big fan of the 1790s.)

WHICH DOGS SHOULD WEAR CLOTHES?

Wrestling with your Saint Bernard to get that tight frilly dress on isn't too practical. But how can Chihuahua parents resist those tiny argyle sweaters when their pups are shivering in the cold winter chill? Some breeds are more fit to be dressed than others. Here's a list of some dogs that should be bundled up when the winter winds blow.

Small Dogs

Boston terrier
Bichon frise
Brussels griffon
Cairn terrier
Cavalier King Charles spaniel
Chihuahua
Chinese crested
English toy spaniel
French bulldog
Havanese
Italian greyhound
Jack Russell terrier
Japanese Chin
Maltese
Miniature pinscher
Miniature dachshund
Miniature schnauzer
Norfolk terrier
Norwich terrier
Papillon
Patterdale terrier
Pekingese
Pembroke Welsh corgi
Pomeranian
Pug
Shih Tzu
Silky terrier
Schipperke
Scottish terrier
Sealyham terrier
Skye terrier
Swedish Vallhund
Tibetan spaniel
Toy fox terrier
Toy poodle
Toy American Eskimo
Toy Mexican hairless
West Highland white terrier
Yorkshire terrier

Short-Haired Dogs

Afghan
American Staffordshire bull terrier
Australian cattle dog
Basenji
Basset hound
Beagle
Belgian Laekenois
Belgian Malinois
Black and tan coonhound
Border terrier
Boxer
Bracco italiano
Bull terrier—standard
Bulldog
Catahoula leopard dog
Chesapeake Bay retriever
Dalmatian
Doberman pinscher
Foxhound—American
Foxhound—English
French bulldog
German shorthaired pointer
Greyhound
Harrier
Jack Russell terrier
Labrador retriever
Manchester terrier—standard
Parson Russell terrier
Pharaoh hound
Plott hound
Pointer
Pug
Shiba Inu
Shih Tzu
Staffordshire bull terrier
Vizsla
Weimaraner
West Highland white terrier
Whippet

What About Shoes and Boots?

If the shoe fits, that doesn't always mean wear it. That isn't to say I haven't splurged on a pair of shoes or two for myself, but Lucky, fortunately, doesn't share my footwear fetish. And thank Dog, because that's another expense I do not need. Furthermore, shoes and boots are completely unnecessary in a dog's everyday life—and let's be honest; if you already had all that padding on your feet you wouldn't wear your Uggs, either.

So unless you plan on making a quick trip to the Alps or Everest or a trek through the Amazon terrain, keep the boots on your own two feet and away from your dog's four furry foundations! This is one way in which it's definitely better for him to go *au naturel*.

Many dog owners in America and other developed nations like Japan started dolling up their dogs in sweaters and boots as early as the nineteenth century; from that point on, doggie fashion trends have developed in tandem with human trends. Dog clothing began mainly as a functional accessory and then morphed into elegant ornamentation before becoming the contemporary designer wear that consumers see in dog boutiques across the United States today.

Extreme pup primping really began in the 1920s and '30s. During these decades, dog clothing became an elegant accessory for elite catalogs like Abercrombie & Fitch, which carried tweed and gabardine doggie trench coats, raincoats, angora sweaters, and other luxury accessories for small and large dogs, with prices ranging from fifty cents to a whopping ten dollars. A 1937 Abercrombie & Fitch catalog reads, "In our dog corner, we have gathered the best the world offers for all breeds of dogs . . . Dogs are welcome in our shop and owners will find here an interested, courteous service and all that pertains to dogs." I knew there was a reason I always

THE TRENDS

Designer labels and prints
Rhinestones - BLING
Fluff
Sports jerseys
Polos

Puffy vests
Luxury fabrics/leather
Vinyl
Tutus
Faux fur

Animal prints (ironically)
Plaid
Denim

liked A&F; it's obviously the very sensible attitude they've always had toward canines.

The 1950s introduced yet another emerging pooch fashion trend, characterized by ballerina outfits and other dress-up costume clothing. In the 1950s and '60s pet parents began to favor pocket dogs like miniature poodles and Chihuahuas; people dressed them up in fancy collars and clothes as if their dogs were a walking, barking fashion accessory. Pups were dressed up to match their parents' clothing, and some parents went so far as to dye their dog's hair to match their own. (Lucky has been trying to convince me for some time to dye my hair to match hers. No dice, I tell her. I'm not letting my hair get white a day before it has to.) One of my favorite photos from the 1960s is of silver-screen legend Joan Collins, posing perfectly with her completely pink-dyed poodle—a little much, and something I probably wouldn't consider doing, but *so* indicative of the times. I thank Dog that we in the twenty-first century have realized that pets are far too important to be treated as living designer accessories.

Human fashion in the 1970s was revolutionized by the advent of leisure suits and other casual wear, and this characterized the trends in dogwear as well. Dog fashion remained mainly functional after the 1970s, but many dog boutique owners and even larger chains claim that the demand for trendy and luxurious dog clothing, designs, and accessories has risen dramatically since the early 2000s. Many designers are taking their cues from modern children's clothing: dresses with embellishments, screened tees, swimwear, doggie sunglasses, goggles, and so on. Although Lucky and I can't take all the credit for the explosive surge in doggie designers and designs since our first Paws for Style fashion

Dog Fashion Time Line

Stone Age
Woven clothes to improve hunting and gathering

AD 520
Protective gear for wars, medieval times: collars

1800s
Dresses and collars

1920s and '30s
Trench coats

1950s
Very fancy, pretty, bows, pink dye

1970s
Casual wear, plain sweaters

1999
Paws for Style was designed, and charitable dog events and parties became the newest fashion trend and wave of tomorrow.

Today
Bling and rescuing!

show in 1999, we do believe the buzz we created played an important part in revolutionizing the entire dog fashion industry. It was no longer hip just to dress up your dog and go out; it had to be for a worthy cause.

Doggie Fashion Suggestions

It's not a good idea to pay *too* much attention to doggie fashion, but on those occasions when your pup has to look perfect, try the following ideas.

CASUAL: Hoodies, sweaters, T-shirts, vests
Lucky can't resist a man in a jersey, especially from our man Ralph Lauren. His Tori Polo Shirt or Rugby Jerseys bring both Lucky and me sporty fun; they're cute, they're great for the warmer seasons, and, best of all, they won't break the bank.

COUTURE: Designers, dresses, tuxes, coats
Marc Bouwer does the best faux fur jackets. Not all of us can afford them—but if you can, how about throwing in a donation to a dog charity while you're at it? Jewels also top the list of couture, including companies with their own iced-out line of velvet and rhinestone-encrusted gear. Satin and silk are also for the dogs; "dogtail" dresses and tuxedos are quite chic for special occasions.

FUNCTIONAL: Rain gear, goggles, weather wear
Bring it on, weatherman! I'll never get sick of it raining cats and dogs, since I don't have to worry about Lucky getting cold or wet—we have some fantastic weather-proof gear on hand for whatever the skies may bring.

NECKWEAR

A great way to snazz up your dog for everyday life is simply to use a great-looking collar, leash, scarf, or bandanna. This is the perfect way to doll your furry friend up just enough so he looks dapper but not overdone.

Nowadays, you have your pick of the litter of fab neck gear. Rhinestone collars, chic leather with buckles, charms, silver, and gold—you name it. Whether it's flowers, gems, or a simple sleek accessory, there's something out there to suit your dog's personality. Lucky, for instance, is a glamorous character—she loves the extra attention that she gets with her own Lucky "Diamond" collar on the red carpet.

Lightweight and soft, scarves and bandannas look sweet and don't restrict movement. If you don't mind spending the extra dollar, designers like Pucci and Hermès have some luxurious options. Satin, silk, or even a shimmery cotton look posh. If your dog or your wallet is more the rugged type, a standard red paisley bandanna is always classic. We're used to seeing it on bigger dogs like retrievers and Labs, but there's no such thing as a dog who doesn't look hip in a bandanna.

DYEING, MANICURING, AND PIERCING

Remember, your dogs aren't the ones who want themselves to be extra primped—you are! Try to keep in mind what's comfortable and cool from your pup's point of view.

PIERCING

I have to take a hard line here; I simply cannot condone puncturing your pooch's lovely ears for vanity's sake. If you really *must* adorn your dog with jewelry, forgo the piercing gun and check out the safe alternative: tacky glue and rhinestones. Make sure the glue is safe for your dog (like nail or false eyelash glue), since anything that you try to put on your furry friend's ears stands a good chance of making it into his mouth. Believe it or not, they also make magnetic earrings for dogs—try a flashy pair of hot pink faux diamond earrings that look like flowers if you're feeling particularly glam one day.

HAIR/FUR DYE

Though I would never personally subject Lucky to a coat of many colors, some pups look undeniably cute with a splash of color. Hot pink, blue, and other neons have been popular colors for some small dog owners who have mohawked their pup's do. *Always* make sure you're using dog-safe color that is all natural and nontoxic, and talk to your vet first. There are a number of companies out there that make dye just for animals, so it's best to try one of them first.

MANICURES AND PAWDICURES

Some people won't let their dog out in public without done-up nails—which is a little extreme. But that doesn't mean that once in a while a fabulous nail job can't be a welcome treat. Groomers will do it all: French manicures, standard trimming and polish, or paint of any color of the rainbow. Jeannine Pirro, New York judge and a darling friend of mine, always makes sure her two poodles' nails are polished with a nice pink coat. Lucky and I think it looks kind of silly in the dog park, but it is sweet on special occasions.

HUMAN FAUX PAW: DOG PARK FASHION

Let's be honest: The dog park is a fantastic way to get outside and give your dog some exercise and fresh air, but if you're a single gal looking for a little puppy love it's not wrong to go with ulterior motives in mind. And even if you're not, you never know who you'll run into when you leave the house—so for a twenty-first-century dog owner, it's imperative to make at least a tiny effort to look presentable. As Mom always said back in Chagrin Falls, never leave home without lipstick in your pocket. You never know who you'll meet at the dog run.

The key to a day at the dog park really is comfort—nothing clingy, tight, or unpredictable (no wardrobe malfunctions, please). As long as you keep it comfortably chic, you'll be ready to face a run-in with any potential beau/belle—or random ex.

And come on, ladies—no heels! There's nothing worse than a gal wobbling around on too-tall stems, trying to look active and unsuspicious. A woman wearing heels at a

Be a Pro Dog Walker!

Hey, you're at the dog park anyway—there's no reason not to make a little cash while you're at it. Dogs are healthier and happier when they hang out with other dogs, so why not do well by doing good? Just make sure you keep the number of dogs low enough that you can hold on to the leashes firmly and pay close attention, and don't mix big dogs with little dogs; the big ones can hurt the little ones even when they just mean to be playing. Spread the word about your new dog-walking business, and next thing you know, you'll be the talk of the dog park.

dog park looks like she's hoping for a little more than just a nice romp with her pup—whether she is or not!

So remember the basics: casual bottom; simple, form-fitting top; comfy shoes. And most important, your dog.

DOGGIE BAG HOLDERS

When nature calls, don't be caught being unfashionable. Get organized with a doggie bag holder—they now come in a spectrum of colors and designs; I've seen egg-shaped dispensers in metallic hues, bone-shaped plastic dispensers, and mini–purse dispensers in different patterns (skull and crossbones, hearts, paw prints), all of which clip right onto your key chain. Check out animalfair.com for additional ideas.

GOING GREEN

With the green movement taking over globally, it seems as if we're destined to go back to the future, reacquainting ourselves with the use of natural resources (wind, the sun) for energy. Although I don't foresee dogs wearing clothing and designs made of leaves and twigs, I do believe natural and organic materials will replace many of the synthetics currently used. Perhaps the next humanitarian dog fashion charity event trend will be "Saving Animals and the Planet They Wear"!

Every Dog Has Its Day

At the end of the day, a dog is a dog! And as much as we want to indulge our canine counterparts with the finer treats life has to offer, pure joy to a dog is socializing and playing at the local park or dog run, drinking plenty of water, consuming healthy meals, joining parents on a daily walk, and a cozy home where a sleeping dog can lie.

My hope and dream is that this book will help motivate every pet-friendly reader and animal enthusiast to get involved with animal rescue, find needy animals homes, and work to make every shelter a no-kill shelter. There are many ways to help in your own neighborhoods. Many communities have a local SPCA (the Society for the Prevention of Cruelty to Animals is a generic term for any group that wants to help animals), local humane society (Humane Society of America is a national group doing amazing things, but your local humane society does not have the budget or PR and needs your support), or small shelter in desperate need of volunteers and donations. The easiest way to find your local animal-aid organizations is to search for them on the Internet or ask your local veterinarian. Many of the shelters have lists of important items they need but can't afford. Any donations of time, supplies, or money are greatly appreciated.

The most important action on the donor's part is to do research before making a gift! Make sure you know where you are donating before pledging. Call the organization and ask as many questions as you need. It is your money and you have the right to know where it is going. Look for organizations that pledge to help the animals in your own community! By targeting each community one at a time, eventually the rescue outreach will create a huge wave from coast to coast. You can do your part by making informed decisions to save the lives of innocent animals.

Here are some ways you can help local animals in need.

1. Consider being a foster parent to a pet in transition. There are many local organizations that specialize in placing animals in loving, temporary homes.
2. Do you know how to sew, knit, or crochet? You could make and donate sweaters, blankets, or even toys to help keep the animals cozy and entertained while awaiting adoption.
3. Throw a party! You can introduce your friends to your local humane society or SPCA and then ask for donations. You'd be surprised how generous people can be after a few glasses of wine . . .
4. Use the power of your vote! Let your local and state representatives know that caring for animals is a priority for you. Write an e-mail that clearly states your views and forward it to your friends and acquaintances to pass on.
5. Volunteer to use your special skills to support your local shelter. Can you design a flyer, write an article, or analyze a legal brief? These (and many other) skills can be invaluable to an underfunded and understaffed nonprofit.
6. Be vigilant! Pay attention when you see signs of animal abuse and report suspicions to an animal protection agency.
7. Be generous! Monetary donations to the general operating funds of local organizations keep the shelters alive. The holidays are a great time to make a gift.
8. Consider adoption and check out your local shelter. Many of these animals have suffered terribly and desperately need your love.
9. Join up! Become a member of an SPCA, humane society, or another local shelter in your community. Many offer newsletters and invitations to events where you can meet other animal lovers in your area.
10. Persuade your friends and co-workers to join you!

Since she came into my life, Lucky has definitely rescued me in many more ways than I've rescued her. With your help and the help of others, every dog in America can be Lucky enough to find a safe and loving home. Dog bless!

Acknowledgments

I would like to thank everyone who helped me to understand just how "Lucky" I am. It's hard to know where to start, but I need to start at the beginning: my family. My mom and dad—if it weren't for them, I would not be so lucky to be on this earth, realizing my dreams and loving every minute of it. Thanks to my five sisters; my aunt Diane; Pepper, my first dog; Tibby and Tiggy, my cats growing up. Thanks, too, to Mary Brosnahan, executive director of Coalition for the Homeless (people and children), for if I did not volunteer for her organization I would never have felt comfortable walking into the Animal Care and Control of New York City homeless animal shelter to adopt Pasha, my Russian Blue cat. Thanks to fabulous dog trainer Bash Dibra, who dropped off at my door "Chloe"—the beautiful homeless Maltese who later became Lucky Diamond! Pasha and Lucky inspired me to launch *Animal Fair* in 1999 to help the 12 million animals in shelters find a home. Thanks to the terrific team at *Animal Fair*—Renay Smith, Pete Carter, Micky Flores, Maria Pepin, Samantha Abernathy—and everyone who helped with this book. Thanks to all the great folks at Ballantine: Libby McGuire, Kim Hovey, Theresa Zoro, Sarina Evan, Kristin Fassler, Katie O'Callaghan, Vincent La Scala, Lea Beresford, and most especially to my two editors: Judy Sternlight, who had the forethought and wisdom to buy this book, and Jill Schwartzman, whose passion and dedication made this dream into a reality. Thanks to Jeff Kleinman of Folio Literary Management, my book agent from my hometown of Chagrin Falls, Ohio; my funny, always-missing editorial assistant David Andrejko; and, of course, the extraordinary Joel Derfner, who made this book hum! Thanks to all the people in the world who have adopted animals, who work at shelters, volunteer at shelters, and donate to shelters: all those people who love animals and inspire others to do the same. I'm forever grateful to everyone who's touched my life—and—oh my gosh!—anyone who actually buys this book!

About the Author

Wendy Diamond is the author of *How to Understand Men Through Their Dogs* and *How to Understand Women Through Their Cats* and chief pet officer of *Animal Fair* magazine and website. She is a pet-lifestyle expert on the *Today* show, CBS's *Greatest American Dog*, and many other television shows. She lives in New York City, where she is a tireless advocate for animal rescue and welfare.

www.wendydiamond.com

About the Type

This book was set in Aldus, a typeface created by the German typographer Hermann Zapf in 1954 for the Stempel foundry. Aldus was designed as a companion to his Palatino typefaces. Palatino was originally designed as a display typeface, but also became popular as a textface. Believing Palatino was too bold for text, Zapf designed Aldus at a lighter weight, more suitable for text setting. The typeface is named for the fifteenth-century Italian printer and publisher Aldus Manutius.